The
Cactus
Stabbers

THE
CACTUS
STABBERS
and other bizarre encounters and reflections

JEFF LUCAS

CWR

Dedication

And this one's for Diane and Nigel,
with love.

My thanks to the editor of Christianity Magazine, *where versions of many of these pieces were first published. And, as ever, to the patient and professional team at CWR, who continue to be such a joy to work with – special thanks to Lynette Brooks and Mark Baker. As always, my love and appreciation to my wife Kay, who faithfully shares the ups, downs, laughter and tears of my rather strange Christian journey. I've encountered a lot of people around the world, but she's still the kindest person I've ever met.*

Contents

Preface

I've flown more than three million miles in the last few years. I've got the facial features to prove it. Constant air travel obviously ages one prematurely, as was confirmed a couple of weeks ago by a rather blunt conversation at the end of a church service. Looking at my wife, Kay, and then glancing at me, a lady remarked, 'She's worn a lot better than you, hasn't she?' It's true. Kay is often mistaken for my daughter, which doesn't exactly cheer me up, especially when she doesn't make a move to correct the misapprehension. But whether it's due to continuous jet lag, dehydration, the stress of being in the emotional black holes that are airports (where nobody over the age of twelve really wants to be, and the place where everyone is because they want to be somewhere else) or just because I've scoffed too many mid-flight peanuts, I look older than I am.

I'm not flying nearly so much these days, not least because of the damage to the environment, as well as the damage to my face: I'd like to look a little less like Lazarus (before Jesus came by).

But although I probably need to get a mortgage to offset my carbon footprint (and don't write me a furious email of complaint, I take that seriously, hence the changes) I am grateful for the experience of criss-crossing the world, Bible in hand. Well, Bible in the overhead baggage compartment.

I've seen so many different expressions of the Church.

In one heady month, I spoke at a Baptist General Assembly where suit and tie was most definitely the thing, a youth conference thronging with hipsters where suit and tie most definitely was not, a charismatic high Anglican retreat where a priest dashed around the conference centre dampening the furniture with holy water, a Salvation Army convocation where I was forced to dance with a rather insistent single lady (you'll read about that later in this book), and a high energy charismatic worship conference where every female on the stage looked like a junior supermodel and the chaps could have auditioned for One Direction. I ate puddings for England at an Irish gathering of Methodists, listened to a baffling number of prophecies at a Welsh Pentecostal conference, and was serenaded in five-part harmony by a lovely group of Mennonites, although, to be brutally honest, I didn't realise that the song was in lieu of paying my expenses, so it was a rather pricey little ditty. It's been rich, educational and, at times, utterly bewildering.

But in the process I've met some amazing, heroic, confusing, lovely, and in some cases, irritating and even profoundly unkind people. My travels have nudged me into hope and joy, thrilled with the privilege of being part of the Christian Church, and have at times edged me into despair and tempted me to think that the Church is sheltering too many mean-spirited, petty souls. I've occasionally thought about forming a one-man escape committee to get out of the whole Church world, and then just when I start digging the tunnel, something wonderfully head and heart-turning happens that makes me fall in love with her – the Church –

all over again. And then God frequently uses a devastatingly effective tactic on me when I feel like walking away from faith and faith communities because of the idiotic behavior of Christians. He just lets me ponder my own idiotic behaviour for a second or two, and *voilà*, the bags I packed to go are unpacked once more.

I'm glad to report that the close encounters of a positive kind greatly outnumber the negative. Sure, there are mean and, dare I say it, silly Christian people out there (and I say that with some qualification and authority, because, lest you didn't get it the first time a full sentence back, I can be both mean and silly myself), but the good news is that there are so many beautiful souls, most of them unheralded and undiscovered. I've even met a few people who are surely superheroes who are living a double life. Quietly moving among us as unassuming, even timid creatures, they are epically brave, and staggeringly self-sacrificing, but they live as they do without fanfare or fuss. They inspire me and shame me in turn.

So allow me to introduce a few of them to you. No air travel will be required on your part (I bet you're greatly relieved). But in the pages that follow I'd like to introduce you to people like lion-hearted Isla, smiling Robin, Peter, who, like ET, desperately needed to phone home, and dancing Eva. You'll meet gracious Larry, who will help us to make sense of Margaret Thatcher. Intrigued? I do hope so.

And in addition to meeting some interesting people, we'll pop into some locations that might currently be unfamiliar. The Australian outback, seething with critters that would like to kill you. A boisterous glory march in a Salvation Army citadel. The sweaty locker room of a seedy strip club.

And I'll share a couple of confessions that I have not gone public with before, such as why it is that I find Jesus to be so profoundly disappointing. Put that stone down if you will, and give me a chance to explain.

I hope that as we travel together through the medium of these pages, you'll smile, find hope, grace, inspiration, and even shed a tear here and there. Together, we'll ponder the most fascinating specimen on earth: the human being.

With love,

Jeff

1 The cactus stabbers

Staying overnight at a bed and breakfast in Australia recently, Kay and I found the room pleasant, the bed comfortable, but the breakfast was really rather awkward.

We began the day parked around a large kitchen table shared with the other guests. The sprawling oak table was laden with home-cooked treats guaranteed to shatter the will of the hardiest dieter, which I am not. Piping hot fresh ground coffee. A stack of fluffy pancakes. It seemed rude not to eat three of those heavenly cranberry muffins, and I'm extremely polite. The food was an utter delight. The awkwardness came from the company.

Our little breakfast gaggle included a couple of wildly enthusiastic evangelists. Their white-hot passion was undoubted and quite unnerving. With no idea that we were believers, their eyes glowed with joy as they breathlessly chattered away about their vital mission to save the world.

No details were spared. I tried to concentrate on the moral perplexities of reaching for a fourth muffin while in the company of strangers, but to no avail: I had to give them my full attention, so animated were they. On holiday, they were even cutting their break short so they could hurry back home to resume their work. And their aims were lofty – nothing less than community transformation was their goal. Their words were sliced with urgency, fueled by passion. They were even planning a float for a local carnival parade, to encourage others to come into the fold and join their mission. And this talkative pair were far more than just talk. They even bore some physical scars with pride, delighted to have suffered for their cause. But they made little of their struggles, and insisted that the pain was nothing compared to the surpassing privilege of being involved in their beloved work.

They were cactus stabbers.

Yes, you read that correctly.

Show them a cactus, and they'll show the cactus a knife.

I know … some further explanation is required.

Their locality in the Australian outback is infested with *Opuntia robusta*, the wheel cactus, a prickly, fast-growing thug of a species that overruns everything in its path. It spreads at an alarming speed, and creates all kinds of problems for animals, including hindering them from grazing. The species has been officially declared a noxious weed in Australia, and has contributed to the loss of billions of dollars due to the damage it inflicts. It is truly a menace. It has to die.

And so our excited new friends were on a mission, not to save souls, but to inject those rubbery foes with the cacti equivalent of weed-killer. Their work was extremely hard graft – the spiny cactus fights back, as the livid scars on their arms confirmed. Undeterred, they had declared all-out war on those wretched triffids. In cactus terms, they are serial killers.

I was impressed by their white hot zeal as they talked on so animatedly, and felt the stirrings of an inkling to jab a rubber plant or two myself. Passion is contagious. Having never contemplated assaulting cacti before, I was surprised by my own interest.

But I also felt quietly ashamed.

I used to be quite the evangelist myself, years ago. My youthful enthusiasm didn't win any prizes for subtlety, but my mantra was simple: I was not ashamed of the gospel. I had a message about a tree that carried the poison of fallenness, the tree of the knowledge of good and evil, and about another, better tree, one planted at Calvary, the cross of Christ. Anyone with the misfortune of sitting next to me on a plane was considered a worthy target for my 'sharing', which usually meant that they were subjected to my breathless monologue. I was high on enthusiasm and crassness in equal measure, and was quite oblivious to the fact the person sitting next to me in seat 32B was (a) asleep, having swallowed a dangerous number of pills, so desperate were they to escape me (b) equipped with earplugs, or (c) pleading with the flight attendant to ask if a parachute was available for them, or if an ejector seat could be made available for me, pronto.

But as I stirred my porridge and heard that the fixated pair, who loathed those pesky plants and loved annihilating them, had even taken early retirement, enabling them to volunteer more time to their work, I wondered: why had all gone relatively quiet on the gospel front for me? Why am I no longer quite so vocal about my faith? In terms of evangelism, have I lost my voice?

How come they made more noise about their genocidal approach to plants than I made of my convictions about eternity?

Superficially, I had *some* answers to the question about my evangelistic quietness. For one thing, I'm in reaction, swinging pendulum-like away from the button-holing, script reading monologues that I used to subject people to. We all tend to think that we're reasonably balanced, but the truth is that we are not centred in truth, but are living in reaction to what has gone before. Generally, we're extremists, veering away at speed from an excess that is equally if not more excessive at the opposite end of the spectrum. That said, I also acknowledge my lack of subtlety, and I don't want to go back to rattling on like a salvation salesman on Duracells, rushing to proffer answers before anyone has had the chance to ask any questions. My quietness is the fruit of maturity, I try to insist, thereby sanctifying my silence. I'm more grown up now.

Besides, I've heard a few sermons where the famous quote, 'Preach the gospel and if necessary, use words' has been used. Excellent. That perfectly justifies me staying tight lipped: I just need to quietly live the Christian life, demonstrating good *works*, but never feeling the need to offer good *words*.

But as I dug deeper and meandered around the mysterious, shadowy caverns of my heart and mind, I discovered something that I find very difficult to confess here. I realised that there were times when, subconsciously, *I didn't actually want people to become Christians.*

There. I've said it. Again, postpone the stoning for a few moments, if you please. A further explanation is tricky if I'm dodging bricks.

I've gone through seasons when the fish symbol beloved of believers apparently symbolized the piranha; when so many Christians acted like predators with razor sharp teeth, I didn't want to have a hand in creating yet another one of the most dangerous of species – an unkind zealot armed with a Bible and a sense that they're on a mission from God.

Then there were periods when so many Christians I encountered seemed to be just a little disjointed, tilted into unattractive oddness by their faith. Did I really want to lead someone else into a potential twilight zone of weirdness if they embraced the way of Christian discipleship?

And my heart weighed heavy for those – too many of them – for whom being a Christian was an intolerable burden. They spend their days shoved around by a barrage of insistent oughts, shoulds and should nots, hotly and desperately in pursuit of a purpose-driven life. Laden down with angst, they lug their faith around like a dead weight. I didn't want to unwittingly sentence others to become like them.

Of course, my silence is anything but golden. I still believe that Jesus, far more than a ticket to eternal bliss, is exclusively the way to find true life today and tomorrow, as He shows us what being healthily human is all about. And if our churches breed strange, stinging, anxious apprentices, then we must ask what's wrong with our message, because, rather obviously, there's nothing wrong with Jesus. On the contrary, He still offers relief to the burdened, not the addition of life-sapping weight.

And so my breakfast encounter with the cactus stabbers brought me challenge, and clarity too. I want to renew my confidence in the gospel. It's lamentable that there are followers of Jesus who are hostile, odd, and agitated, but that doesn't make the truth any less true. I'd like to be a little more ready, willing and able to not only live a *life* that points to Christ, but gently speak *words* that light the pathway towards Him too.

And as for that famous quote about preaching the gospel ('if necessary, use words'), it is commonly attributed to St. Francis of Assisi, famous not only for chatting with squirrels, but also for giving everything away to the poor. When you offer the clothes off your back – literally – like St. Francis did, it's not likely that you're going to be short of opportunities to share Jesus. This saying is not a call to silence, but to action that is far more arresting than a breathless torrent of evangelistic spiel.

As our breakfast ended, and I wished our new friends well in their ongoing murderous mission, I decided that I want to embrace a little more passion and clarity of my own. In not wanting to be brash about Jesus, I don't want to be ashamed of Him. I decided that I'd like to have a winsome enthusiasm that sparks interest, not fear. And although I'm not going to abuse the fact that the person sitting next to me on the plane is truly a captive audience (the ejector seat and parachute not actually being available), I'd like to genuinely offer a prayer of availability when I get on the plane, inviting God to allow me to be of help to a fellow passenger, rather than just provide me with an empty seat next to me so that I can stretch out more. A little more comfort would be nice, but a genuine moment of service would be better.

I'm not going to dash out and slap a fish sticker on the back of my car, but I'd like to be more willing today to stick my head up above the postmodern parapet and be glad to be known as one of Jesus' friends, without fear.

And speaking of fear, I'm just a little concerned.

My rubber plant's looking decidedly nervous.

Go ahead, *Ficus elastica*. Make my day.

2 The happy camper 1

God is a camper.

And I most certainly am not. I've tried the outdoorsy life, lured by the thought of the gentle pitter-patter of rain on canvas, the happy late night chatter around a roaring camp fire, and the cocooning warmth of a sleeping bag, all snuggly and comforting. In reality, our soggy kindling woodenly refused to emit a flame, prompting me to wish I'd taken a blowtorch along; the zip on my sleeping bag broke, exposing me to the horrid chill that seeps into one's bones in the small hours, and the rain came down in a monsoon-like deluge that would have made even Noah nervous.

Life in the wild can be just that – very wild. I've been chased by an inquisitive raccoon, and even hotly pursued by an irritated duck, which obviously had some anger management issues.

Just putting the tent up is stressful, and can threaten

family harmony. My tent of choice was surely created by designers who were inspired by dark forces. Other campers sometimes find themselves with a spare peg after erecting the tent. I usually have a tent *pole* or two left over, which does not suggest enduring stability. Family harmony was threatened by family hilarity, as my nearest and dearest mocked my tent erecting attempts at high volume.

Of course, before launching into actually putting the tent up, it's important to locate the right site. The ground should be solid, but not concrete. Camping too close to trees might be less than helpful, as folks don't take too kindly to forest fires – not that this would be likely with our damp wood. But to pitch one's tent in the wrong place can be perilous. Arriving late at a site after dark, we inadvertently set our tent up beside a golf course. The next morning, irrationally thrilled by the thought of brewing tea on a propane stove, I was oblivious to the Japanese golfers who were teeing off just yards away. I soon became aware of their presence, receiving a golf ball driven at speed in a rather tender spot. Much screaming from me followed, as did much apologetic bowing from them, but I suffered no permanent damage, and went on to father two children. But I've decided. A happy camper I most certainly am not.

But God is very much into camping. Almost half of the book of Exodus is an instruction manual for putting up a tent – the tabernacle. Every detail is set out with painstaking clarity, and is even repeated. With pillars of cloud and fire acting like an ancient GPS system, the divine wilderness trekker called His people to journey with Him, pausing where He paused, and moving on with Him whenever He chose to break camp.

The God of the Hebrews was the One who was and is always going somewhere. Back in Moses' day, 'gods' were treated like vending machines. If you needed a bumper crop, good weather, or the blessing of a baby, then you'd sacrifice to the god who specialised in agriculture, sun, or fertility. The process was simple, predictable even: insert coin (or offering) in the slot at the temple/altar/shrine, and then await response hopefully. But there was no sense of divinity with a direction. And then the Lord revealed Himself to Moses as a traveller, one with a plan and a purpose, not just exclusively for Israel, but for the whole earth. Later, when the Jewish Temple was built, the tabernacle was scrapped, but there was always a sense that God's 'proper' abode was a tent.

And then Jesus came, and in the language of John's Gospel, 'he pitched his tent in our neighbourhood'. He called time on the Temple, which had become a static monument, languishing in tradition, squatting in exclusivism, and insisted that He was now replacing its rituals with Himself, that He was now the Way. Bricks and mortar gone, deal cancelled, replaced by a Person.

He invited people to follow Him, not promising an easy, predictable excursion with a pre-established itinerary, but a hike that could involve pain, persecution and even death. The gospel call is not to ask Jesus into our hearts – Him coming to where we are, but rather that we become His followers and friends, who go with Him where He's going. And it's not just that we travel through the scenery of changing circumstances, but into the personal metamorphosis that He brings. We're called to be a people on the move, forward into change, onward into being changed.

But are we? Perhaps some of us have settled into sameness for a while. Or we tend to think more about past expeditions rather than fresh, unexplored trails that are up ahead, more preoccupied with nostalgia than dreams. If we wonder if we're still discovering, consider this: when was the last time we admitted that we were wrong? Settlers often snuggle down into the warm myth that they are invariably right.

Asked to give a benediction at a Christian event recently, I decided to replace the usual words of blessing with a less orthodox parting shot:

'God says, "I'm off. Who's coming?"'

It's time to pack, not park. We have hooked ourselves onto a rope with a trekking, camping God. Let's go.

3 The happy camper 2

I know. I wrote about camping before, just one chapter ago, and here we are again.

Obviously I have issues.

Before embarking on the Christian journey, I was warned that the pathway ahead might be littered with myriad perils. While martyrdom or outright persecution was unlikely, I would likely face ridicule and misunderstanding. Some of my friends would probably disappear, put off by my newly found faith. This trek might be costly, an uphill climb. But there was one unavoidable element of Christian discipleship that nobody warned me about, which is probably a good thing, because if I'd known, I might have opted for Buddhism instead.

Camping.

Within weeks of deciding to follow Christ, I found myself at a youth camp, ensconced in a wigwam-like tent for two whole weeks. I went there feeling somewhat jaundiced, because my pre-conversion experiences in the great outdoors weren't great.

But despite my initial hesitation, that youth camp was really quite marvellous. Fragile, fledgling decisions were galvanised, even if I was a little over-enthusiastic as a new convert. Every evening service during the camp would end with an 'altar call', and I responded every night, whatever the issue. If the preacher was calling for martyrs, missionaries, or throwing out the net in the hope of recruiting a new leader for the 'Women Aglow' group, I'd dash forward, offering myself to any opportunity for service.

I repented of a few things that were not actually sin. I made impossible promises and pledges to God that I had no hope of following through on. I even composed a couple of songs that I 'performed' for the entire camp during one of the evening gatherings. They listened, smiled, even applauded, but were probably praying for my early death. The songs I wrote were likely tuneless and laden down with horrid clichés:

Thank You Jesus for dying on the tree
I was bound but now I'm free
Love that's deeper than the sea
And my response is to give You … me

You get the drift.

We used to end the evening by sharing 'testimonies' – stories of how God had helped us that day or week. Again, I think that my zeal cancelled out any shred of thoughtful intelligence, as I regaled the gathered group with stories of how God had said, acted, intervened and done things – whereas in realty He had done nothing of the sort. I was grateful to find my lost socks in the laundry area, but it's doubtful that the Lord sent a junior angel on a specific mission to help me to (a) locate the missing socks and (b) help me to glorify Him for their wondrous recovery.

But amidst the youthful over-exuberance and quite a lot of silliness, there's no doubt that attending that camp solidified my initial conversion experience, not least because I spent a fortnight hanging out with others who had made the same choice. This was definitely peer-pressure of the most positive and helpful kind.

And then I graduated from tents to chalets, and became involved with Spring Harvest for over three decades. That too was a delight. The word 'chalet' was at times a little misleading for American friends who crossed the pond to see what the event was all about. Told that they'd be staying in a *chalet*, some imagined a luxurious pine log construction, where they'd be waited on by a blonde Swedish sister called Olga. There'd be a log fire, a sauna, an opportunity to whip each other with twigs following the sauna, and even bears in them there woods.

It wasn't *that* kind of chalet.

And then I went to so many services during my time with Spring Harvest that I began to feel sorry for God, who attends a lot of services, meetings, small groups, gatherings, and conferences, omnipresence having its drawbacks. Our day would begin with a leadership team prayer gathering which included a 'thought' for the day. Then we went on to the morning Bible study, followed by main seminars, optional seminars in the afternoon, another pre-service prayer meeting, a big top celebration event, and sometimes even a late night gathering too. I sang so many songs, I wondered whether I'd disturb the entire site by waking in the middle of the night screaming 'Shine, Jesus, Shine' at the top of my voice.

But it was wonderful, and life altering. At Spring Harvest, I learned that the way my denominational tribe did things was not the only or the best way. I encountered people who loved Jesus greatly, far more than I did by all accounts, but whose style of worship and theology was quite different from my own. I found that Christians can accomplish more together than we can alone, as we campaigned for the Siberian Seven, launched Stop the Traffik, and got behind the initial licensing of Premier Radio.

And then, even though I've mentioned all those meetings, there was a genuine thrill in standing shoulder to shoulder with thousands of other Christians who were melding their voices together in united praise. What a treat for those who faithfully gather, week in, week out, in tiny congregations: to bask in the experience of praising God with so many other members of their Christian family.

Spring Harvest gave me an opportunity to examine my theology rigorously, to ask questions without fear of being labelled, to establish lifelong, veteran friendships that continue to this day, and to celebrate the broad family that is the Church. There, innovative ideas were forged. Faith was strengthened. Authentic hope was replenished. Laughter and tears were shared.

Of course, none of this should come as a surprise. God is not only a festival goer, but a festival organiser too, as the Hebrew feasts and festivals amply demonstrate. Those ancient people of God, so gifted at sliding into amnesia and forgetting their story and purpose, were summoned together frequently and inconveniently to help them recall what was most important.

Of course, there are some of the 'bah humbug' types who insist that all this event going is a waste of time, that we should concentrate our efforts on working at the coalface of our own localities. I utterly disagree. Events like Spring Harvest, ONE Event, and Soul Survivor can be far more than high energy knees ups that distract us from our purpose, but can effectively equip us to fulfil our purpose with fresh determination and energy.

Camping. I still don't like sleeping bags or soggy groundsheets.

And those chalets were not quite like those inhabited by the rich and famous on the snow white hillsides of Switzerland.

But tents and chalets have been major stop-offs in my Christian hike so far, and I'm glad.

4 Isla

Sometimes, important things slip from my mind. A person at church asks me for prayer, and panic sets in because I realise that I can't remember their name. Resorting to saying, 'I just pray for ... this man', 'this woman that you love', or even, 'my brother' is unconvincing and definitely unhelpful, especially if the person is requesting prayer because they feel insignificant because nobody ever notices them or remembers their name. I forget my keys, the directions to where I'm going, and, oh yes, I forget that I'm going to live forever.

That's right. The Easter message has nothing to do with grinning bunnies or chocolate. It includes the truth that, in Christ, life doesn't stop when the muscle of our heart does. We're destined, not just for endless existence, but eternal life. We don't know much about what that will look like, but we can be assured that it won't involve angels endlessly strumming harps while drifting around on candy-floss clouds, or the predictability of a billion year-long prayer meeting. Though the details are sketchy, this much is wonderfully true: we will be together, and that togetherness will include Jesus, face to face, the centre of attention.

But that truth can be eclipsed, not only by busyness, but also by yet another pendulum swing reaction. We've rightly reacted to the false notion that the Christian message is just about getting people signed up for a blissful forever. We've realised that the kingdom is very much now, but in doing so we might have neglected the truth that it is also not yet. That there's more. And eternity had slipped my mind, until a friend and neighbour, Isla, nudged my memory last week. It was a much-needed nudge.

Isla is a Christian, and she's lived an adventurous life. Married to Gary, who has climbed some of the highest mountains in the world, she has travelled the planet and seen some amazing sights. Recently she found herself viewing a less inspiring spot, the inside of an oncology ward. All treatment options were explored, but ultimately Isla received the dreaded news that she was dying of cancer. She put up the bravest of fights, even submitting herself to experimental treatment in an attempt to send packing the dispassionate bully that is cancer. She refused to panic in the shadow of that bully, but stared it down with calm, dignified faith. There were times when it seemed that the cancer might have been tamed, cowered by the genius of the tireless medics. But recently doctors told her that there was nothing more to be done. All options had been exhausted. They sent Isla home to die.

Recently, we stopped by to see Isla. Weakened and aged by the disease, she was battling nausea and pain. But a beautiful light shone in the few minutes that we shared, banishing the shadow that death casts. The light source was in a woman who was staring at impending death, but did so with such enormous courage and hope. We asked how we might pray for Isla; she selflessly said she wanted God to strengthen her loved ones, because she knew that her passing would bring such heartbreak and grief. There was not a shred of self-pity, not a hint of angry rage.

And then it was time for us to leave. For a moment, it felt awkward, because we were leaving town, and we all knew that this would likely be the last time we saw each other. I kissed her on the cheek, thanked her for being such a wonderful neighbour, and then took a deep breath: 'Isla, it's not goodbye, is it? We all know it's just goodnight. Whatever happens, we'll see you in the morning. Resurrection morning.' She smiled and nodded, her eyes bright. We prayed together, affirming that she was safe, totally secure with Jesus.

And now she is with Him. The news came through that Isla had passed. But not only has she lived well, but died well, able to say goodbye. That doesn't happen as often as we might think. Sometimes, when Christians are dying, they and others around them go into denial. Thinking that to concede that death might be imminent seems like they are denying their faith claim for healing, they spend their last days denying what is obvious. Tragically, some die with a sense of failure. This is outrageous; enduring the pain of terminal disease is more than enough, without this additional burden of irrational and quite undeserved shame. I know of one dear man who, having been given a terminal diagnosis, refused to let his church know, because he didn't want to disappoint the intercessors. He passed with a lingering feeling that he had let the side down.

And for many, there is no beautiful, tearful farewell. If I was going on a long journey that involved separation from my friends and family, I'd love to be able to let them know that I'm off, and bid them goodbye for now. Isla did just that.

The gospel is about life *before* death, as we pray, serve, give and work to see the kingdom come on earth. But it's also about life *after* death, as the new Jerusalem comes down to a renewed earth, and a new kind of living rolls out. This much is true: pain, cancer, and tears won't be there, because Jesus will be. Sadness will be evicted permanently. I know, it can sound too good to be true, but the message is not less true because it's so very, very good. That's why we call it the *good* news.

As often as we can, let's remind each other of this truly good and great news: death is beaten, vanquished in Christ. Too often we forget. I had, until a brave lady who lived next door reminded me. Her name is still Isla, and because Christ was and is, she still is too. She climbed the Everest of death and found that, at the summit, there is no flag, but rather a cross, and an empty tomb.

Isla. Now that's one name that won't slip my mind.

5 Robin

Smiling doesn't come easily to me. It's not that I'm Victor Meldrew with a Bible, a practiced misery with facial features permanently arranged in a gloomy scowl. And I'm not a dedicatedly angry type who views life as a negative safari, ever hunting for more opportunities to frown. It's just that my smile is somewhat lopsided, which makes me self-conscious.

I blame my mother, and not just for bequeathing me her genes. Sending me off on a childhood shopping errand, she provided a plastic carrier bag that got tangled in the front wheels of my bike. This enabled me to fly without a ticket, which is what I did, right over the handlebars. Landing with a sickening crunch that gifted me with a nose that can see around corners, I have been cursed with a wonky grin ever since. Not only does this mean that I get nervous when having my photo taken, but it has also provoked some interesting conversations when I flash my crooked grin in public.

'Jeff, may I ask, have you ever had a stroke?' asked one forthright lady after I'd delivered a sermon that was probably not about thoughtfulness and tact.

'I haven't,' I replied, confused. 'Why do you ask?' Perhaps sensing what was to come, I inwardly wrestled with the temptation to say that I was just seriously ugly, and ask her what her excuse was, which would have been enjoyable, but most un-Christian. And so I remained silent, usually the best policy in these situations.

Her reply was swift and blunt, which is a shame.

'It's just that, when you smile, only one side of your face goes up.' My distorted features collapsed into a frown. No wonder I hesitate before releasing my incongruous grin upon the world.

Robin has no such hesitation about smiling. Distinguished and dapper in his blazer and tie, he was the officially appointed photographer for a church anniversary weekend where I was the guest speaker. As out-of-town guests, we didn't know anybody at the church, and felt the wintry draught of being the strangers at the party; but when Robin greeted us, the sun came out. His consistent grin was broad, cheeky without the hint of a leer, and utterly welcoming. So bright was that smile, I asked him about it. He explained that, for him, a warm smile is not just a response to something good, but a daily choice.

He explained. 'Years ago, I was sitting in a barber's shop opposite a church building. As the Christians emerged from their weekly Bible study, everyone in the barber's remarked that they didn't want to be like those dour church folks with their vinegary, holier-than-thou expressions. Listening to the murmuring that day, I made a life choice. I decided that, as a follower of Jesus myself, I would smile.' And so he does. A lot.

Now, don't think that Robin is a superficial soul, or someone for whom life has been easy to the point of seeming unfair. On the contrary, he lost his beloved wife of fifty-eight years, Joan, just three years ago, after her decade-long battle with Parkinson's disease and dementia. And his daughter Celia suffered a brain tumour at the age of twenty-two, just after she qualified to be a nurse. A brilliant young woman, now she is confined to the full time residential care that her condition demands. Despite being paralysed from the waist down, she is a bright, inspirational soul – a source of joy and encouragement to all who meet her: happily, the apple has not fallen far from the proverbial tree. And so Robin, a retired civil engineer, hasn't been spared the winters of life. But he has decided to choose his attitude, daily. And in about two seconds, that choice made us feel completely at home. His conscious monitoring of his facial arrangement changed our evening.

The tiniest actions change the world, and not just the actions that are celebrated. When the late, great Rosa Parks decided that she was not going to be relegated to the 'blacks only' section at the back of the bus, she couldn't have known that her small protest would fuel the revolution that was the Civil Rights Movement.

But there are many other small choices that are not noticeably history making, but nevertheless quietly change the world each day.

Noticing. Saying please. Saying thank you. Listening in a world awash with talking. Opening a door. Tipping a little extra. Paying a genuine compliment. Helping a lost tourist. Offering a handshake or a hug. Apologising, quickly, without hesitation or qualification. Wishing someone a good day, and meaning it, even if your day is going badly. Encouraging people, and being specific about it, not just saying 'well done', but saying *what* was well done. Sending a hand-written note. Bringing a gift to a dinner party. Helping with the washing up after dinner.

And yes, offering a smile. And perhaps another small choice might be pausing for thought before we ask potentially offensive questions, like the unsubtle enquiry about my stroke.

Of course, the dear lady meant no ill, and to her credit, as soon as the words tumbled out of her mouth, she realised that her question and comment might be a little rude. I was about to smile to reassure her, but happily I refrained. My attempt at a warm grin might have prompted her to scream in shock, dial 999 and summon an ambulance.

6 Popeye Lucas

Whenever the new year comes around, I catch myself pondering potential resolutions. This year, I decided to go easy on myself. Rather than aspiring to lofty, impossible goals that will demand steely discipline and resolute dedication, I settled on some more reachable objectives. I cut back my bassoon playing, I haven't spoken Cantonese so far, and I will diligently eat plenty of chocolate. As a non-musical chocolate lover who has never owned a bassoon and who only speaks English, I have a moderate chance of success. And so I am thinking about changing my name from Jeff to Popeye. As in Popeye the Sailor Man. As names go, it's unusual, but pertinent.

Popeye is a cartoon character, a product of the 1930s. Played by the late, great Robin Williams in the movie version, he has a gruff voice, a very strange giggly laugh, a clay pipe, and a passion for a rather drab looking young lady called

Olive Oyl, who looked like a stick insect with her greasy hair pulled back into a missionary bun. I never understood the attraction. That girl needed a cheeseburger. A makeover. And some shampoo. Yet Popeye was smitten with her.

Despite his strange taste in women, Popeye could do most things, especially when he ate his beloved spinach. With his piston-like muscles and that versatile pipe (which could even propel him into space) he was a sailor-saviour, rescuing Olive, and occasionally, the world, from all manner of calamities. The muscly chap also had some strange eating habits, including consuming his spinach through his pipe, which is a tad unusual and not a habit I'd recommend. Tobacco flavoured spinach. Yuck.

But there was one thing that Popeye just could *not* do. He could not be other than what he was. He could not change. He even sang a lament about it, a sad serenade to his resignation that he was sentenced to sameness.

'I yam what I yam, and that's all I yam. I'm Popeye the Sailor Man,' he sang, with a haunting, depressing lilt.

And so the reason for my name change, from Jeff to Popeye? Simple: I've realised that I have largely stopped changing.

Nearly four decades of pastoral leadership has taught me this unpalatable truth: people rarely change. That includes Christians.

I know. That statement is the opposite of the Christian message, which is not just about a few minor behavioural amendments here and there, or the creation of a sin-management system. It's about the birth of a whole new species of humanity as the newly created person in Christ, fuelled by the indwelling Spirit, becomes more Jesus-like. It's a message about metamorphosis, which is why the question, 'What would Jesus do?' is helpful, but inadequate. Not only do we not know what Jesus would actually do in our complex world of myriad ethical choices, but we must know that the gospel calls us not to just engage in the sweaty activity of trying to be like Jesus, but rather we become like Him as He progressively transforms us slowly and gradually, today and tomorrow. We are called to co-operate with Him and His work in us, not just chug away at change, helplessly and hopelessly.

But the cold fact is this: too many of us have turned into old dogs who aren't too keen on learning any new tricks, or leopards that aren't thrilled about losing those spots.

That's not to say that we never ever did change. Conversion brings new values and therefore revises behaviour. In the flush of enthusiasm spawned by first love, we breathlessly abandon some of our old patterns of life. But some of it is only skin deep, a temporary transaction. As new Christians we hastily trawl through our lives, declaring war on the more obvious, lurid behaviours which we rightly judge as being incompatible with Christian discipleship. But having tamed the bigger beasts, we slowly settle down, and wait for the sound of a heavenly trumpet, when everything will be changed in a moment, but in the meantime, not much about us changes in a decade.

What was fluid turns solid. Fresh turns stale. We get weary of the call to endless revising; the preacher's shrill challenge for yet more amendment and deeper commitment wears us out, and so we quietly tune it out. We wonder if *they* will hear the sermon, the *they* being those that really need to hear it, which, we've decided, excludes us.

And then some of us live secretly, bound in chains of addiction, advertising freedom while we languish in the chill of a cell block. We believe the poisonous hiss: this is just the way you are. Face it. Accept your sentence without too much protest. That's life. You're only human. Nothing to be done.

But, even though this is not how we are called to live, the how and why of change are difficult to quantify. As a preacher, I so desperately want to offer seven sure-fire steps to transformation, preferably beginning with the same letter. This much I know: change begins with renewed thinking. It's not just about scrubbing up on the outside.

Scripture views change as something positive: we tend to fuss about what we're not, rather than dream about who we're becoming; subtraction rather than addition. But we are being 'transformed ... from glory to glory' (2 Cor. 3:18, NKJV), says Paul, who himself experienced personal revolution. We tend to focus on pruning; the Spirit is about producing rich, luscious fruit. And of course change results from the supernatural, inner work of the Spirit in us: true change is a sign and a wonder.

So when we make resoultions, let's know that change is not only possible, but, if we will follow Jesus by faith today, it is inevitable. Perhaps that truth will allow us to swing a sledgehammer at the hopelessness that can stop us in our tracks and see a crack appear in the solid mould of what we are.

We *can* change, and so I've changed my mind, and decided against that name change. Popeye Lucas just sounds so wrong. And wrong it is.

7 The baron

At first glance, he looked like a perfectly ordinary chap. I had no idea that he was so immensely powerful. He had developed the ability to control an army without so much as a word. No barked commands needed from him, no parade-growl yell of intimidation. Just a raised eyebrow. A frown. The shake of a head, and they all knew, and would respond accordingly. Obedience without question or hesitation. I glanced again. He was the king of a kingdom.

Scanning the otherwise responsive congregation as I preached, now he stood out like a very sore thumb. Seated six pews back on the left – the place where, I later learned, he always sits, *his* pew – he didn't look too happy. Either he was fighting to digest some food that had passed its sell-by date or he was struggling to agree with what I was saying. Finding his stony expression a little disconcerting, and battling a niggling anxiety that I had inadvertently uttered something quite heretical, I made the mistake common to many preachers, as I tried in vain to draw him into my sermon. Hoping for the merest hint of a smile, or even a nod of affirmation, I looked his way as I spoke. But he just stared straight ahead, arms folded and locked, a grim statue of a man.

Then it dawned on me that I was not the only one interested in his expression. A good number of the congregation were listening to *me*, but had one eye on *him*. Some were actually leaning forward to catch a glimpse of his reactions. I wondered. Why the fascination with him and his facial arrangements?

That's when I realised that they, like me, were tensely waiting for a cue. Obviously quite a significant player in that church, this man's opinion was esteemed, his influence heavy, and so his response to this new speaker – namely me – was a matter of great importance to almost everyone in the place. If he looked unamused, then their expressions turned frosty. If he appeared concerned, raising a perturbed eyebrow or offering even a hint of a frown, then where his eyebrows went, others' followed. Whatever he did, they followed suit. I guessed that if he had smiled, then they would have relaxed, sighed with relief, and smiled too. I said I guessed. He never did get around to smiling.

Inwardly, I made a diagnosis, which later conversation proved to be right. He was a baron.

Barons are everywhere. You'll find them in every social context: committees, parent-teacher associations, clubs, families, and of course, churches. Barons are control freaks on steroids. They like their coffee, their homes, their marriages and their churches to be neatly arranged around their preferences; their environment neatly folded to their precise specifications. Some are recognised leaders, most are not, but all of them certainly know how to get people to follow them.

Barons will use a variety of tactics to get exactly what they want.

Some are gifted exaggerators, spinning stories of mass discontent to create fear. Often they claim to represent the majority, insisting that they have a mandate for their opinion. 'Everyone's leaving the church,' said one baroness who boasted a PhD in control.

'Really?,' I enquired, genuinely alarmed at the potential exodus, but wanting to know exactly who was about to exit. 'Well', she nodded gravely, as if the place was emptying even as we spoke, 'lots of people are leaving the church.'

'May I enquire as to exactly who is leaving?'

'Two or three people ...'

'Please tell me who.'

'Well I don't like what is going on here, and if it doesn't change soon, *I* am leaving the church.' I resisted the temptation to do a little joyful dance.

Some control by undisguised bullying. If they're leaders, they hiss that any dissent is divisive disloyalty, and that an opinion contrary to theirs is a betrayal, an insult to their integrity. The statement, 'You're a threat to our unity' is as devastatingly effective as 'You're a witch' is to an unfortunate soul who is strapped into a ducking stool by a river.

Still other barons use quiet, meek stealth, controlling as they don an apparently fragile demeanour. Concerned that confronting them would destroy them, everyone creeps around them, and the sound of crunchy eggshells underfoot is deafening. And then there are the baronial control freaks who use syrupy pleasantness to get their way. They smile, and seem impossibly kind; to cross them would feel quite wrong, so nice are they. But behind the smarmy grin is a calculating mind.

And *church* barons have the ultimate weapon. The G-factor. G for God.

When control freaks produce the God card from up their sleeve, they usually hold a winning hand. When you insist that God has spoken to you, or that you're surely representing what He thinks, you play the ultimate trump card. Few can challenge you, and those that do don't stand much chance of winning.

But even though barons may be powerful, they are not usually brave in battle. When they're in danger of losing an argument, they often cancel the conversation by jumping up and walking out. This is an ingenious device, because it gives the impression that they are being highly principled in their retreat, when they're actually just running for cover. So what if it's a cowardly stunt? Whatever works.

Barons. Perhaps you know one. Perhaps you are one.

Meanwhile, back at the church where I was preaching, the baron sat rigidly unmoved, and the people around him were become tenser by the moment. Seeing this bizarre scenario playing out before me, I momentarily considered confronting the situation head on, by sharing an old chestnut:

'Knock, knock.'

'Who's there?'

'Control freak, and quickly now, you're supposed to say, "Control freak who?"'

But then I looked at his set jaw, and then at those who sat pensively around him. And I thought better of it.

8 Baby George

My encounters with the British royal family have been rather limited. I'd love to be able to say that I've spent many happy days hobnobbing with the Windsors, but, alas, it's just not true. I *have* been inside Buckingham Palace, and I have even had tea on the back lawn, but I paid for the tour. And I have been within about ten feet of Queen Elizabeth, but I'm not proud of the encounter. Riding in her annual birthday parade, she trotted down the Mall resplendent on a horse while a young pre-teen friend and I ran alongside yelling expletives. Hopefully she didn't hear me. And if she did, mercifully, she didn't order me to be executed for treason.

But I did meet Prince Philip in person once, when he came to a youth club where I was a member. Much ado was made of his visit, including the construction of a special toilet that was reserved exclusively for the princely bottom. We were told that, when the great man arrived, we were to carry on doing whatever we were doing, because His Highness wanted to see the club in full function. If he approached us, whatever we were doing, we were to bow. When he finally swept in, flanked by a large entourage, I was bouncing on a trampoline, and to my horror, he headed straight towards me. With a brief greeting, he moved on, my hand never even shaking his. I'd like to say we've been lifelong friends since then, but it's obviously not so.

Despite my not being acquainted with the royals, I was still one of the worldwide throng who were delighted at the arrival of young Prince George, son of William and Kate, and probable future king. As he was carried across the hospital threshold to blink in the flashlights of the paparazzi for the first time, he obediently lifted a little finger as if to wave. These royals know how to do their stuff from the earliest age. Twitter went crazy, with 25,000 tweets a minute greeting royal boy George's arrival. But watching the event unfolding from America was fascinating, because the interest here was overwhelming, and I wondered why. The USA has Independence Day, the day when our Yankee cousins celebrate the vanquishing of the British. This is a proud republic. So why should they be even vaguely interested in the birth of a distant future king?

Perhaps there are a number of reasons. Babies are cute, and turn many of us into cooing, infant-talking idiots when we encounter them. Then there's a fascination that many Americans have with anything British, for which I'm grateful, having been treated with irrational kindness ever since I've lived here. And there's also our global *Hello!* and *OK!* dominated culture, with its insatiable thirst to know everything about celebrities, that surely fuels the fuss.

But I've been wondering – is the American interest with royalty a sign of something deeper? In short, do all humans everywhere long for a king? Were we designed to be ruled?

Whatever Eden was, it's portrayed as a kingdom, a place of order where a good, righteous Ruler reigned. It was paradise, not because the first couple lived it to the max with no moral boundaries and a 'just do it' hedonistic philosophy, but because order and peace was theirs because the good King was in residence. Surely humanity has been purposely designed with a desire, even a need, to be ruled over by a righteous King who will reign with love and justice, and make true shalom a reality.

Sometimes that hunger can lead us to stumble, as happened to Israel back in old Samuel's time. Dissatisfied with the King they couldn't touch and see, they insisted that they needed a visible King who would lead them into battle, just like the nations that surrounded them. The need for royalty led them to bad choices. But then, when Jesus came, He had one main message that He kept repeating – the good news that the kingdom of God was here. Far from just offering a ticket to somewhere else for ever, He talked about the rule and reign of the King and His kingdom, here and now, and yet a reign to be fully established and consummated later. Living with a bowed knee and a surrendered heart – far from being abnormal, for this we were made. Perhaps the American fascination endorses that idea. Wherever in the world we live, and whatever our politics, we've been created to be subjects.

Meanwhile, back at the trampoline, I learned another

couple of lessons. Royals sometimes disappoint: Prince Philip never did use that specially built toilet. And there was a lesson about etiquette as well. It certainly isn't easy to bow and bounce at the same time.

9 Gracious Mr. Wiggins

Christians don't arm themselves with crowbars. At least, not usually. But on a crisp autumnal day, Kathleen Folden, a truck driver, marched into our local museum and began smashing the glass that surrounded a painting by a Stanford-based artist, Enrique Chagoya. The irate Kathleen yelled, 'How can you desecrate my Lord?' as she tore into the painting. Within minutes, she was arrested, and was photographed wearing a t-shirt emblazoned with a caption: 'My Saviour is tougher than nails!'

The painting targeted for the attack caused national controversy. Fox News gave extensive coverage to the reactions from some local Christians who were incensed about what they saw as a 'blasphemous, pornographic work'. And the image was certainly unsettling. Two men, one of them looking Christlike, engaged in a sex act. Placard waving protesters gathered outside the museum. The artist was barraged by hundreds of vitriolic emails from outraged Christians, some of which, incredibly, included death threats. Stanford University was forced to hire security to protect the beleaguered Chagoya. The internet was rife with Christians tagging the artist as a blasphemous jerk, together with plenty of other names. And then a local pastor, Jonathan Wiggins, received an email from one of his congregation, demanding that he add his voice to the protests. He sprung into action.

After prayer, Wiggins decided to take another, riskier route. He emailed Chagoya with a warm message that can be summarized like this: 'tell me more'. 'I told him that I didn't want to debate him, but just hear him,' said Wiggins, who leads a large, growing congregation in the city. 'I let him know that, whatever his response, we as a church would be praying for him to be blessed every day of his life.'

A remarkable series of email exchanges between the two followed. In what was to become a developing friendship, the artist explained that the character portrayed in the work was not Jesus at all, but was an iconic portrayal of the church. His painting was a response to the outrage of the Catholic paedophile scandals, in which, as he put it, 'the spiritual has been corrupted. Something so precious got corrupted'. If the task of the artist is to confront with the reality of the way things are, Chagoya was being faithful to his calling.

The conversation continued with honesty and warmth, the two became friends, and when Pastor Wiggins shared the email dialogue with his church – with permission from Chagoya – he received a standing ovation from the congregation. Knowing that he was walking into risky territory because of the strong feelings about the painting, Pastor Wiggins had been accountable, and had previously discussed his dialogue with the deacons of the church, who with tears, insisted that he was doing the right thing. Wiggins was relieved and grateful for their wholehearted support. 'They said that this is what Jesus would do. Go for it!'

The story speaks to us when we are tempted to react rather than respond. We rush to a rant, rather than reaching out for dialogue. Leaping to judgment rather than pausing to listen and understand, we damn others without dialogue. And then, when we feel that others are being spiteful, we often respond with spite. But Pastor Wiggins' example shows us that everyone has a story. That doesn't necessarily legitimize what they do or how they behave, but as we listen, and offer unexpected friendship, we may come to understand why they feel as they do. The softly spoken enquiry, 'tell me more' can be an invitation that can win over rather than alienate.

Kathleen Folden, the crowbar swinging lady, later explained that she had been 'incensed' by the painting. She was ordered to pay a large fine and sentenced to probation. She was to later set up a website 'explaining' her actions that day.

In a later statement to his congregation, Pastor Wiggins clarified his motives for reaching out to Chagoya. 'Of course, as a Christian, I'd love to see him come to Christ. But whatever his response is, I'll be proud and honoured to have him as a friend for the rest of my life.' And Wiggins invited the artist to create another painting, one that actually portrayed Jesus, and did so in a way that captures the beauty of His love. Chagoya asked the minister to offer some advice about how he should paint Jesus, and then later wrote, 'I see Him in the beautiful descriptions of Christ that you sent me'. A stunning portrait now hangs in the church building, a gift to the church from the artist. A lifelong friendship has been forged. An artist has discovered a new vision, not only of Jesus, but also of His Church. And a congregation has learned to demonstrate resilient love – a love that is truly tougher than nails. Thank God for gracious Mr. Wiggins.

10 Peter & Riekie

It's a phrase that's bandied about too frequently in Christian circles: 'the Lord told me'. We've all met those breathlessly confident souls who imply that everything they do is directed by the voice of God. The Almighty is not just on speaking terms with them, but is apparently very chatty; the cosmic choreographer, seemingly issuing commands about the minute details of their everyday life. It's difficult to question them, because, like the Blues Brothers, they're on a mission from God, so they're rather insistent about their frequent revelations. Sometimes they affirm that God has told them to even do bizarre and illogical things, which stifles any discussion or potential disagreement. Those who insist that God is an extra-terrestrial tweeter can inflict great pain. I remember being in a church service when an enthusiastic lady grabbed a guitar and shared a song that, she declared, the Lord had given her the night before, and now He was instructing her to share it. Eleven unpoetic verses and a chorus that involved some high-pitched shrieking later, the shell-shocked congregation privately concluded that, if the Lord had indeed given the lady that song, it was probably because He didn't want it. But sometimes the pain goes deeper than the eardrums.

I've been given more than my fair share of 'prophecies' that were utterly incomprehensible, which is awkward when you're on the receiving end. It's difficult to know how to respond when a wannabe prophet announces that he has seen a picture of a one-legged Japanese bassoonist who is balancing a bowl of custard on his head, and then enquires, 'Does this mean anything to you?' It does indeed mean something: someone should call the NHS helpline immediately. And others have been casualties of what might have just been well-meaning over-enthusiasm, and they have been directed, diagnosed, corrected or condemned by people who insist that they are talking to others because God has been talking to them.

All of which means that I have tended to veer towards cynicism when people announce that God has told them something, which is an unhelpful overreaction. Healthy *skepticism* is useful when people announce that they've heard the word of the Lord, because we need to test and prove what is offered, rather than swallowing it wholesale. Spirituality is a call to abandon everything, but not to kiss our brains goodbye. But I want to stay open to God speaking to me through others, and be available to those subtle nudges, impressions, hunches and prompts that are sometimes the direct work of the Holy Spirit in me, lest I miss a genuine whisper from heaven. And that might be very bad indeed, as I learned when I met Peter and Riekie. For them, a hint from heaven was literally a life-saver.

A bright, joyful couple, now living in Spain, Peter and Riekie's easy smiles and relaxed demeanour could suggest that they've had a carefree life, which they have not. Sharing during a retreat that I led, Riekie described her childhood as a catalogue of sexual abuse. Her description was stark: 'Growing up, abuse seemed to follow me.' And then came the dark day when, home alone, Riekie was raped by a man who had been doing some casual work around their house. Riekie's one-year-old child was in the next room, and she feared for the safety of her baby, and said so. The rapist paused his assault to make sure that the child was safe, but then continued the terrible attack.

But it was then that the telephone rang. And rang again. And again.

It was Peter, who was at work. There was absolutely no reason for him to be calling – Riekie was supposed to be out collecting the children in the late afternoon school run, but Peter could not escape a persistent, overwhelming urge to phone home. And so he just kept calling. When there was no reply, Peter hung up, and called again. The rapist, distracted by the constant jangling of the phone, abandoned the assault and made his escape. Other rapes had occurred in the area, some resulting in terrible injuries inflicted by screwdrivers, others resulting in AIDS infection; some victims had been murdered. Riekie wonders what her fate might have been if Peter had not responded to that inner nudge when he did.

The day before the incident (which was anything but incidental), Peter had felt that he should specifically pray that God would protect Riekie from rape: and then for twenty-one long years that followed that terrible day, he had wrestled with anger towards God because the attack had happened. And then, during the retreat, it suddenly dawned on him: he had been the answer to his own prayer. Obviously, the answer was not as he would have wanted it – he would have preferred that the attack had never happened in the first place – but the internal nudge brought intervention into what might have been an even worse tragedy.

But lest all of this seems a little too neat, let's acknowledge that God doesn't always speak, intervene, or rescue. The telephone doesn't always ring at the vital moment. Today awful things will happen, not only to good people, but to God's people. Peter and Riekie's story doesn't guarantee that God will always be the knight in shining armour; no telephone rang during the traumatic episodes in her childhood. Some of you reading this might feel a touch or a surge of anger as I share this story, because you have suffered terrible abuse, and no phone rang. I don't know why that is, but I know this for sure: it was certainly not your fault. Even answered prayer presents difficulty, because every answer begs the question, 'then why was that other plea for help not answered?'. Nevertheless, Peter's obedience to that nudge teaches me this: God speaks. ET is famous for the phrase, 'phone home'. But if God wants to whisper it, or give me an inkling, a hint, or a nudge, then I'd like to be someone who has ears to hear, and a readiness to respond.

11 Jesus is profoundly disappointing

It's been brewing in me for a while, this desire to come clean. Sometimes the unthinkable notion just simmers away benignly on the edge of my brain, posing little threat to my peace. Occasionally the simmer boils over into a full-blown rage, and drives me to stomp around the house, hotly pursued by my own portable raincloud, urging me to bunch my fists in heaven-directed anger rather than fold my hands together in prayer. But even though the thought seems laced with betrayal, and some will surely misunderstand, here goes ...

After four decades of being a Christian, I confess this: I am very disappointed with Jesus.

Some years ago Philip Yancey produced his provocatively titled book, *Disappointment with God*. His publisher was nervous, and predictably there were plenty of honest-to-

God critics who insisted that a Christian book shouldn't be titled so honestly. Nevertheless, it became a bestseller, giving credence to this uncomfortable truth that there are plenty of Christians out there who share this most awkward feeling: Jesus is profoundly disappointing.

So why do I feel so?

For one thing, He hasn't delivered as anticipated. When I signed up by praying that 'sinner's' prayer, I heard that God speaks as well as saves, so I assumed that He would be a lot more chatty than He has been. The early days were bewildering and utterly confusing, but I always thought that this was because I was like an amateur radio operator; surely I would soon develop a fibre-optic crystal-clear conversation with Him, instead of what often feels like faltering, ancient AOL dial-up, with all that crackling and spluttering and frustrating reception that I generally experience. Frankly, there were days – months even – when I thought that the connection had gone down for good. And my ability to tune in hasn't improved greatly. I've questioned the idea that prayer is a conversation, as if every day is punctuated with dialogue, a back and forth flow of comments and ideas. For me, prayer is most often what I say to Him, and very, very occasionally what He says to me – or at least what I *think* He says to me. Very disappointing, because I was expecting to live life like a pilot constantly in chat with air traffic control.

And then I'm disappointed by what seems to be His indifference, or at least, His apparent unwillingness to intervene, especially in the situations that I care about the most. I don't want Him to zap the hungry mum turned shoplifter with a billion volts of instant judgment, or even pass out a puncture to the driver who is two miles per hour over the limit, especially if that driver happens to be me. But I *do* want Him to torch the wild-eye religious maniacs in Sudan, who plan to whip the mother of a newborn with a hundred lashes, and then take her out and hang her by the neck until she's dead. That's a great use for a cosmic flame-thrower. And I want Him to catch the little two year old who slipped off of a rock in the swollen river down the road recently, and have Him change the outcome of that terrible day, when a cold, lifeless body was recovered two hours later. I've asked Him a thousand times to banish the evil dementia that clouds my dear Mum's mind by day, and sometimes terrifies her by night, but He has not. The fog of confusion and fear is thickening for her, and I watch helplessly, and more often than not just don't ask Him to heal her anymore. And it's not that I don't believe He can do it. He's God, so He can. But He hasn't, and probably won't. I don't doubt His power, just His willingness.

And it's not that I only want Him to play a hand in preventing the pointless and tragic. It would have been nice if He had bared His arm in the cause of making my day-to-day life a little more comfortable, like providing me with a parking space in the busy high street, teeming with shoppers and clogged with cars today.

While I'm at it, I'm disappointed in what He has done – or not done – in me. I'd hoped for transformation, not just mild revision. I was expecting slow but measurable metamorphosis into a sleek, spiritual athlete, able to streak ahead, impervious of spiteful critics, swatting aside pesky temptations like flies. And I thought that the burly Goliath of doubt, the one that stomped around largely unchallenged in my earlier years, if not slain, would at least be tamed or downsized. Some preachers and writers make spiritual growth sound like a straight line trek on a clearly marked pathway; as long as you play by the rules, and don't wander off to wallow in any tempting sinful bogs, then you'll grow incrementally. But it's not been that way for me. My pathway has been more of the 'two steps forward, five steps back, pop up a dead-end cul-de-sac, and then park for three weeks and eat cheeseburgers' kind of journey.

I'm disappointed that I don't understand Jesus more these days. I wanted the flimsy slogans that I once leaned on to not just evaporate, but be replaced with something more solid, more substantial. But the more I travel, the less I get it, and the less I get Him.

And when it comes to disappointment, don't even get me started on the Church. Okay, *I* got me started, so I'll finish, quickly. Suffice to say that there are countless wonderful souls; quiet servants who change the world daily, unnoticed and uncelebrated. But there are enough quick-on-the-draw-with-clichés types to send me into despair, and yet more disappointment. Just today I heard of yet another Christian leader who has fallen out with his church, and so is starting another one just down the road, in direct and obvious competition. He's actively targeting the members of his former church, especially the big givers. He's recruiting by demonizing the congregation he led for decades. And, even more depressingly, he's rewriting the story of what has happened, casting himself as the lonely, rejected hero. Challenged in his first church because of his domineering leadership, his oppressive attitude towards women, and his bullying of staff, he is now insisting that he has been wounded in a religious power struggle, but now, as a fearless wilderness wanderer, he will rise again and create a radical, male-focused, city-saving congregation. And the sad truth is that he believes his own version of the story, and he'll keep rewriting and shaping the narrative as the days go by. Disappointing too is the naive simplicity of the people who will believe the fairy tale and follow him without much question.

Of course, my disappointment with Jesus shouldn't come as a surprise, to me or those who hear my confession. Let's be honest. God has always been something of a disappointment.

Furious Jonah was incensed that God could possibly like, never mind love and forgive, the hated people of Ninevah. So he went overboard, stomped off and booked a cruise, and then went overboard again, literally. Moody but faithful Jeremiah accused the Almighty of being a deceiver. Elijah ran for his life and then prayed for death – a rather illogical way to do things – and then repeatedly bleated about his disappointment with God, and with the way things had turned out. And the psalmist wails repeatedly: 'Why do you stand afar off? Why? Where are you? Where have you been?' Scripture doesn't airbrush out those who went through times when they found God deeply disappointing.

And then came Jesus. And the disappointment continued.

Ask the Pharisees. They made loud speeches about divorce, adultery, and fasting, hoping to corral Him into agreeing with them. When He sat down for supper with untouchables, they hoped that their pious sounding murmurings would make Him change His mind as well as His dining arrangements. They were gravely disappointed. He resisted their pressure to conform. He wouldn't dance to their tune. Disappointing indeed.

A rich and religious power broker came to Jesus, hoping to grab eternal life without losing his grip on the cash. Deal or no deal? He went away sad. Disappointed.

Then there were the quiet power brokers, like Salome, the mother of disciples James and John. Mistaken in her view that Jesus was about to set up rebellious thrones in Jerusalem City, she came to Jesus with a proposition: how about a throne for my boys, one at your right, one at your left? Application refused. Request denied. And instead of a glorious throne, cups of suffering proffered all round. Most disappointing.

After the resurrection, two forlorn travellers trudged the seven mile trek to Emmaus. Hearts heavy because of the execution of Jesus, they were so exhausted by disappointment that they failed to recognize Him as He suddenly joined them. As He questioned them, they offered the prayer frequently prayed by the disappointed ones: 'We had hoped.'

And then even after the resurrection, the disciples had to realise that Jesus was not going to fulfil their cherished hopes and dreams. Once again on the hunt for a Messiah who would scatter the hated Romans, they put in another request: Lord will you at this time restore the kingdom to Israel? But it was not to be, at least not as they viewed it. Jesus was working to a much bigger plan.

So now that my disappointment is confessed, what now?

One way forward is to distil my expectations from His promises. It's unfair to blame God for not doing what He has never promised to do in the first place. My feeling disappointed doesn't mean that I'm right to feel so; just because someone doesn't live up to my hopes and expectations doesn't automatically make me right and them wrong.

So 20/20 vision was never assured. Instead Scripture tells me that I see 'through a glass, darkly' (1 Cor. 13:12), to borrow King James Version language. Instant intervention, even if I yelled, 'In the name of Jesus' at shrill volume, was never pledged either. Not only do we do faith on a broken, bloody, sin-marred earth, but we do so as agents of a kingdom that is not yet fully here. We are assured that pain and injustice will be banished *ultimately*, but not *imminently*. Every prayer is not answered with a quick yes. If we doubt that, ask Jesus, He knows. A request repeated three times in Gethsemane was turned down flat. And I do think that God has better things to do than be guarding parking spaces for His people. That said, the notion that He doesn't exist for my comfort and benefit dies hard, even though it is so absurd to suggest that angels are deployed to help out with my parking arrangements.

And then even when I see the Church at her petty, carping worst, I shouldn't be surprised, because in-the-process flawed humans are involved. In Scripture, the Church is never portrayed as a perfect gaggle of grinning people who have arrived. The Early Church stank of humanity; glorious fellowship mixed with the grime of jealousy, misunderstandings, immorality, drunkenness (during communion, no less), betrayal, and hypocrisy. Often people say wistfully that they wish that modern churches could just be like the Early Church. Not me. A realistic approach to Church is important, especially for the dreamy visionaries who expect Church to be breathtakingly exciting on a weekly basis. Reality diffuses the potential of disappointment.

Allowing Jesus to be who He really is, rather than trying to call customer services because He has not fulfilled my false expectations, is vital. Because I am disappointed with the Jesus that I *anticipated* does not make me disappointed with the Jesus who *is*.

Of course, this doesn't solve all the issues, which is uncomfortable for me. I desperately want to resolve the tensions, tidy things up, tie up all the loose ends. There are still genuine questions and disappointments, and perhaps eternity alone will begin to bring a dawning of answers to most of them.

What I will say is this: forty years on, Jesus is quite unlike what I've sometimes wanted Him to be, but faith says that He has been all I've needed. I need to bring my disappointment, whether it is truly with Him, or with the Jesus that I imagined He might be, and determine to follow Him anyway. And that probably comes down not to what I feel, but a commitment to what I believe is true. Earlier we saw that the refused prayer in Gethsemane, the repeated request that He might be spared the terrors of the cross, was turned down. Disappointing indeed. What hope must spring in the soul of the condemned prisoner on the executioner's gurney, as the telephone from the governor's office suddenly rings? This might be the sound of a last minute reprieve. And what stifling despair and disappointment must be theirs when they realise that it's just the signal to go ahead with the grisly procedure. But from the depths of disappointment, knowing that the cross was the only way, Jesus walked calmly in the hands of the arresting party. Disappointment didn't dissuade Him from faithfulness.

Earlier, in a season when others were deserting Jesus, the disciples, wrestling with their own broken hopes and surfacing fears, made an honest statement when He asked if they were leaving too. Perhaps with a shrug of the shoulder and a look of quiet resignation, they said, 'to whom shall we go? You have the words of eternal life'.

And that's not a bad prayer to pray.

12 Strange fire

The charismatic movement includes around 500 million people worldwide – about 25% of those who profess to be Christian. That's rather a lot of people. And according to one Christian leader, John MacArthur, they are all guilty of blaspheming the Holy Spirit. Strong words indeed.

MacArthur, a famed champion of conservative reformed evangelicals, launched his scurrilous attack during 'Strange Fire', a conference attended by around 3,000 and broadcast into 127 countries. He is a figure of considerable influence, the author of 150 books, including a study Bible that has sold over a million copies.

MacArthur's comments were anything but moderate. Dismissing charismatics as being part of the explosive growth of a false Church, he insisted that '90% of charismatics align themselves with the prosperity gospel', a ridiculous notion that follows the folly of the BBC, who recently suggested that Pentecostals teach that consulting medical help is wrong. Four decades of travel around the world, and being with countless Pentecostals and charismatics, has taught me this: very few of them have any sympathy with the extremes of 'name it and claim it' prosperity teaching.

Tragically, MacArthur even refuses to acknowledge that Christians of a charismatic persuasion have made any contribution in serving their communities, insisting that 'there has been zero social benefit from the charismatic movement'. In a stroke, millions who quietly serve in homelessness projects, food banks, debt counselling services, as street pastors, and in scores of other social initiatives were consigned to the dumpster. But MacArthur went further, adding the ultimate insult to injury. He even insisted that, in many cases, he was not speaking out against fellow Christians, as he believes that the charismatic movement is 'made up largely of non-Christians'. It's helpful to finally have someone on the earth who can make such a clear judgment about who is in, and who is out of the kingdom of God.

Understandably, outrage followed. But in the wake of the furore, while totally disagreeing with MacArthur, I am wondering if these deeply unpleasant, prejudicial comments have been made partly because those of us who call ourselves charismatic have refused to clean our own house. We should not be surprised when someone like MacArthur comes along, not with a broom, but a bulldozer, and with gross caricaturing tries to knock the whole house down. Perhaps our silence has fuelled his intemperate verbosity.

I am a charismatic Christian. I am deeply grateful for my Pentecostal roots. If it were not for the winsome witness of the Pentecostal church where I found Christ, I wonder where I would be now. Their sense of anticipation about God captivated me: when they prayed, they expected something to happen; there was nothing sleepy or mediocre about their faith. Indifferent to sleepy, musty, theory-centred religion, I was excited by their excitement. I continue to be one who is grateful for the ongoing active work of the Holy Spirit, including the supernatural gifts, not just because my experience demands it, but because Scripture insists upon it. God empowers His people, and I find no hint in Scripture to suggest that this empowering does not continue. In my four decades of faith, my life has been punctuated with some moments when, wonderfully and arrestingly, God spoke to me through prophecy. I believe that God still heals today, although I must immediately add a caveat: He certainly does not heal as often as we would like, or even as often as some claim.

And there are plenty of ridiculous ideas that attach themselves to the subject of healing. Just today Facebook was rife with conversation about how healing 'is in the atonement of Christ', and therefore a cancer sufferer might be well-advised to abandon his treatment. Not only is this guilt-inducing tosh, but wrenches Scripture totally out of context. But the notion still does the rounds, and people get hurt or disappointed as a result.

And so rather than lobbing a few salvos back at MacArthur, we'd do better to acknowledge that there certainly are some issues that charismatics must face and some extremes that need urgent correction. Too many predictive prophecies have been made, but when the promised outcome did not come to pass, little more than a quiet cough of embarrassment followed. People have looked for revival that didn't dawn, earthquakes that never produced a tremble, and even marriage partners who never materialised. And in some churches, people 'speak in tongues' and then an 'interpretation' follows, but the congregation are generally aware that the interpretation came from a well-meaning enthusiast, but not from the heart of Almighty God. Any attempt to bring correction can be thwarted with the insistence that we should not quench the Spirit, which is ridiculous. Sometimes bizarre behaviour has been defended as being 'deep', and those who question it are dubbed as superficial, and a fog of Gnosticism – where some claim to have greater revelation – has pervaded. Some of us have put aside our niggling concerns, fearful that we would be dismissed as those who were insensitive or resistant to the moving of God.

I'll go on. In some charismatic gatherings, the ultimate objective is apparently to have a lot of people lying on the floor, allegedly knocked flat by the Spirit, but sometimes helped by heavy handed prayer ministry volunteers who 'assist' God with a little shove. And is the Lord really a divine dentist, providing gold fillings for the faithful? I've never understood the gold filling craze that has done the rounds in some circles. Wouldn't a new tooth be better rather than a metallic filling, even if it is made of twenty-four carat metal? It seems a little like giving a wheel chair user a new set of tyres …

And then there are the extremes of the prosperity movement that I mentioned earlier, where cash giving is related to blessing and especially healing – a tarted up version of the medieval practice of selling indulgences. While the vast majority of Pentecostals and charismatics that I know would totally distance themselves from this unbiblical madness, perhaps we should have made our position clearer. Not that speaking out is so easy. Even in making these comments, I risk the ire, not only of those who want to defend MacArthur, but my charismatic friends who will bristle too.

Nevertheless, I believe that Mr MacArthur is wrong in the tone and content of his 'Strange Fire' accusations. But those of us who call ourselves charismatics are not entirely right.

13 My visit to the strip club

Yesterday, I went to a strip club. I was especially nervous, because it was my very first time. I've lived a sheltered life. I loved my visit, and hope it won't be my last. I'd love to go more regularly.

Outside, a sign painted with busty silhouettes screamed 'GIRLS! GIRLS! GIRLS!' Accessing the place was awkward. Looking around furtively before entering the dimly lit building, I worried that I might be spotted going in. It wouldn't be good to get caught in this act, what with my being a pastor. But my nervousness was tinged with undeniable excitement, my courage bolstered because I was not alone. Joined by a noisy gaggle of boisterous friends, all of us were thirsty for the same thing, hence this hasty boy's outing. I studied the price list on the way in, which warned, helpfully, 'No touching'. Inside, two small stages served as centrepieces, each one boasting a shiny pole. Lighting rigs hung sullenly over the stages, dark, at least when we arrived, set ready to illuminate glistening flesh. In a shadowy corner, a 'VIPs only' section was set aside for semi-private lap dances; a bargain, it said, for just six dollars a song, free drink included. Hard chairs were replaced by couches there; booths offered seclusion and privacy.

We checked out the bar and then, suddenly bold, a couple of us headed straight for the dancer's dressing room, ignoring the scrawled warning on the door: 'No men except for managers.' Bursting in uninvited, I inhaled the sickly, perfume-thick air, and glanced at the family snapshots that festooned a few locker doors. Some pole-dancers have children, and they're working hard to feed them. Languishing in the corner was a chaotic pile of shoes, with high heels that could create altitude sickness. One of the shoes seemed so very small. We fell silent, momentarily ashamed now of our maleness. We knew that those who strut their stuff in those glittery clogs were unlikely to have happy feet, as nightly they squirm and gyrate for men like us, for perspiring punters with ogling eyes. Pinned to one of the lockers was an obscene message penned from one dancer to another.

We walked back into the main performance area. A few threadbare, upholstered chairs were scattered around, black with sweat. Grime seemed to permeate the pores of the place. Gathering on the dance floor, we decided ...

It was time for some action.

It was time for the show to begin.

I know. I need to explain. Ours was a gang of Christian leaders. We were invited to tour the club, out of hours, by the co-owner. A relatively new Christian, he'd decided that this cash cow of his needed to die; the meat-market must close, perhaps, he hoped, to make way for a new church to gather there. His dream is that the club could become a safe place, a house to show and tell good news that another love is on offer, one that gives and doesn't grab, one that offers safety and security, for ever.

Thirty minutes later, fledgling plans hatched and urgent prayers prayed, we emerged back into the sunlight once more. And we all knew that we would never be quite the same again.

Because we visited when the club was closed and otherwise deserted, we didn't meet a dancer, or a client. But those tiny, sparkly shoes gave silent testimony. Those little feet had once been even smaller, perhaps walking barefoot, naked through grass and unashamed, a young child carefree, not knowing then that exploitation was just around the corner.

And back in that dank gloom, a lie was exposed. Here in the place where dancers lose their clothes, a deceptive emperor shed his clothes too. Illicit sex disguises itself, tarts itself up with grand, adult sophistication. It whispers exotic promises, baits the hook with allure. But it's all a tawdry sham. Far from a bargain, the six dollar dance is actually the worse possible deal, for the lap dancer as well as her wide-eyed 'very important person' that is the client. Personhood is actually eroded in their hollow transaction as both are used and become users – he objectifies her for a thrill, she sees him as just another pathetic cash source. In the grubby shadows, the thin veneer of glamour was peeled away to reveal the festering truth: when people are commodified, ugliness reigns. It's purity that's truly gorgeous, faithfulness that's the real stunner.

Our car was very quiet on the ride home, and not just because we were appalled at what we'd seen. Perhaps we all knew the sobering truth: given the right set of circumstances, or a moment of temptation, we too are human beings, well able to pull up a chair for ourselves beside that fetid stage. Whatever hints of holiness we have about us, they are only ours because of grace. Much as we'd like to deny it, those staring men who are club regulars are not so very unlike us. Fastidious about the dirt we see in others, we can be slow to see the grunge in us. If the club is to become a beacon, those who serve there will go as fellow broken, fragile souls, still under construction, rather than holier-than-thous on a pious mission for God.

We're planning many more trips back to the club, hungry and thirsty to see despair kicked out by a bouncer called hope. We want to see dignity where there is degradation; hope where there is nothing but a bleak future with yet more leering eyes and the possibility of another few bucks. Who knows? Perhaps we'll shape one of those brassy poles into a cross; a symbol of condemnation and shame becomes a sign of death but then glorious resurrection. If God helps us, we just can't stay away.

Because it's time.

It's show time.

14 The full time Christian worker

When Mark Greene showed up to speak at Spring Harvest, sporting a fluorescent red badge on his lapel, I was a little nervous. I had abandoned badge wearing years earlier, having worn a variety of Christian adornments, without much success. My silver fish badge meant that my jacket matched the back of my car, but some who spotted it thought that I was a member of the International Confederation of Cod Friers. My dove gave some the impression that I was a pigeon fancier, and my rather more garish and saucer-sized 'Don't be caught dead without Jesus!' badge didn't provoke too many warm conversations, but just meant that some didn't want to be caught either dead or alive anywhere near me, which, on reflection, is not surprising. And I had abandoned my 'Honk if you love Jesus' sticker that had once been stuck resplendent on the back of my car. Someone who loved Jesus very much obviously took my sticker to heart and honked at me repeatedly. Sadly, I forgot that I had placed the sticker there, and my angry response demonstrated that I didn't love Jesus as much as I had thought. So when Mr Greene, who by his own admission looks quite like a Bible-carrying Rowan Atkinson, showed up festooned with his rather garish badge, I feared that he had strayed into rather Bean-esque territory. And I was quite wrong.

Mark's badge boldly declared the initials *FTCW* – the letters standing for 'Full Time Christian Worker'. With great passion and eloquence, Mark preached, calling everyone, regardless of work or vocation, to view themselves as full time agents of the kingdom of God. As Mark, with keen insight and kindness mingled, sought to tear down the mythical divide between so called clergy and laity, I nodded a hearty agreement. This was a vitally needed message. For years there hadn't been too much teaching on faith in the workplace. Christians knew that they weren't supposed to purloin the office pencils, make personal phone calls, have workplace affairs (or any other affairs, come to think of it, regardless of location) and were encouraged to use every opportunity to talk with work colleagues about Jesus. This had not really equipped me for my time in the workplace. Employed by a large, busy London bank as the world's very worst counter clerk, this led to some problems, especially with the chief cashier, whose undisguised disdain for my Christianity meant he insisted on calling me 'God'. Undeterred, I tried to twist every conversation around into an opportunity for evangelism:

Me: I've not been able to balance my till again.

Chief Cashier: Oh, haven't you, God?

Me: Yes. I mean, no. I'm not God, but my till is wrong, which means that I have erred. So it's a jolly good thing that I can be forgiven for my mistakes by the Lord. By the way, would you like to come to …

Chief Cashier: Oh do go away. (Not his precise words, but this is a Christian book.)

Members of the clergy were often guilty of making comments that devalued the workplace and those who spend the vast majority of their lives there. 'Fred is taking up holy orders', gushed one parson. 'We all know he's far too gifted to be accountant,' he smirked, thereby trashing every accountant in the place. And then there was the prevailing notion that being called to be a minister, or even better still, a missionary – because missionaries had to avoid snakes and use awful toilets – meant that you had been given the highest calling, which is quite wrong. The highest calling for us is found as we live according to God's broad plans for us. If being found among the clergy is not what God has planned for you, it's not that you missed the highest calling, you've been spared the wrong one. So I cheered when Mark empowered all to boldly go where most people go every day: to the workplace. And I still cheer. More than once I have desperately tried to convince successful business people to not abandon their workplaces and careers in favour of full time Christian leadership, because they have been raised to believe that the latter is better. I spent ages trying to convince a highly gifted and successful businessman not to abandon his burgeoning career in favour of becoming a Salvation Army officer. If that's what God was asking him to do, then his aspirations were wonderful, and well worth the sacrifice, but I feared that his choices were forged by his upbringing, and the quiet notion that being an officer – a Salvationist clergy equivalent – is the best and most noble way.

But I'm also wondering if the pendulum swing that so often characterises us Christians needs to be balanced just a little. Have we lost the value of those who *do* serve in the church in a full time capacity? Sometimes I've heard it said that they need to get a proper job. In my experience, their job is very proper indeed, in terms of its demands on both time and skills. Church leaders need to multitask as administrators, public speakers, scholars, counsellors, public servants, and be gifted with HR skills that are enviable, seeing as they have to manage a workforce of volunteers who can't be disciplined with a pay cut or fired. They have to be gifted in areas of conflict resolution, especially when those who fall out with each other often insist that God is on *their* side. They frequently work very long hours with compensation that is low enough to bring additional pressures to their already busy lives. And while the New Testament calls all of us to do everything to God's glory, making our work a solid part of our worship, nevertheless there is a nobility given to the calling of 'bishop', together with a great burden of responsibility too.

All of this, of course, was and is precisely Mark's point: that every one of us, wherever we find ourselves among those blessed to be able to work, must know that whatever we do with our time, we do so as agents and worshippers of Jesus, who spent most of His life on earth learning to make the New Testament equivalent of a coffee table.

Full time Christian worker. Now that's a badge worth wearing, and a destiny that's worth embracing.

15 **The crowd**

The man fiddled nervously with his impossibly tight tie. His pristine Sunday morning church attire was slowly strangling him. For a long moment, he stood silent, and then at last, spoke to me without actually looking at me. His unsmiling face chilled words that should have been warm. 'I need to thank you for your ministry, Jeff,' he whispered hesitantly, apparently studying a fascinating object that hovered three feet above my head. He quickly continued, rushing to qualify his positive comment, perhaps before some blasphemous pride was allowed to take root: 'But then we give all the glory to the Lord, don't we? I wouldn't want you to get proud.'

I thanked him, and so wanted to deliver him of his constricting tie, and of his hesitancy to encourage. I desperately wanted him to know that Christian leaders are more likely to succumb to despair than to conceit, to feelings of inadequacy rather than superiority, but he quickly fled, leaving me with a sad realisation. In some churches, there's a famine of encouragement. Faithful, hard working souls live in a suffocating, desolate atmosphere that pervades when appreciation is rare. Working hard in the hope of a final 'well done' that will come when all is said and done as Jesus makes a full appearance, they live shrivelled lives in the meantime. Starved of words that might spur them on, they hobble on. The assumption is that serving God should be reward enough, which is quite wrong, because the God we serve urges us to encourage one another. His encouragement usually comes through His people.

Encouragement transforms, energises, and empowers, as the glorious Olympics and Paralympics of 2012 repeatedly demonstrated. The crowd was the genuine all-rounder of the games, remarkably making a huge impact at every event. Commentators chattered about the home advantage, or the 'fifth man in the boat' that was the crowd. Athletes looked wide eyed, and some openly sobbed as the crowd roared. Some women even sported Wiggins-esque sideburns in support of Sir Bradley – not a usual fashion choice, but effective none the less, as we willed Team GB to win. The deafening choruses of support acted like adrenaline, urging spent muscles and weary hearts on to greater exploits. A German journalist said that the London crowd deserved a gold medal. Sprinter Marlon Devonish, in an anti-doping campaign, announced that the crowd was his only drug. When you have the roar of encouragement that comes from the hearts and throats of thousands, it's not surprising that you surpass yourself.

So why was the crowd the 'X' factor that helped many to medal glory?

More than a wall of noise, surely the crowd met the athletes' primal need that we all share: the need to be noticed, and approved of. We want to be seen, and that's not wrong. When Jesus warned the religious barons of his day about doing religious acrobatics in order to be seen, he was rebuking them for haughty pride, for show-and-tell religion, not for the human need to be noticed just because we're there. We never grow out of that need. As children, we crave the eye and encouraging words of a parent, as we wobble on our bikes, bring home the chaotic painting, or use a toilet successfully. And encouragement is the fuel that can lift our heads through our darker days, when the valley is filled with shadows.

This was poignantly demonstrated at a three day event, a triathlon of sorts, involving incredible physical stamina, steely mental fortitude, and emotional staying power. The demands were gargantuan, and so a team huddled together the night before the event, and their prospects weren't looking good. They were exhausted before they started. And then the next day, the home crowd turned hostile. They switched allegiance, dumped their national hopeful, and cheered for a champion from another land instead. Their chant was an ominous betrayal: 'We have no king but Caesar. Crucify that man'.

And so, on transfiguration mountain, the voice of the great Encourager had spoken loud and clear. 'This is my Son, whom I love; with him I am well pleased. Listen to him!' (Matt. 17:5). That voice had spoken before, just before another battle, this one for forty days and nights; 'This is my

Son, whom I love; with him I am well pleased' (Matt. 3:17). Spurred on by that encouragement, Jesus lived. Urged on by that familiar, encouraging voice, Jesus died.

So go ahead. Make someone's day. Catch them doing something right. Search out the soul who is usually taken for granted. Thank the ticket collector on the train, even if he's shocked because you saw past his function and spied a person. Smile at the traffic warden. Write a note to that Sunday school teacher who has told the big story to countless squirming six year olds for decades; some of them are in their thirties now, but few have come back to thank her. Sometimes she wonders if it's all been worthwhile: put a dent in the lie that she's tempted by, that it's all been a waste of time. Win a gold as an encourager.

And whatever you do, please know how to *receive* encouragement too. Some Christians go into ultra-panic mode when they are confronted with warm appreciation. A lady approached a minister and thanked him for his sermon, which sent him into a spluttering disclaimer, with much pointing to the sky. 'Don't thank me, madam, no, please, the Lord did it, give Him the glory.'

Her reply was insightful, if not terribly encouraging: 'Well, actually, it wasn't *that* good ...'

16 The lovely Eva

I was delighted to be in Australia, despite the disconcerting reality that there are lots of assassins there. Australia is a nation that welcomes tourists, with warm smiles, countless opportunities to toss yet more shrimp on the barbie, discounted Ugg boots (watch out for knock-offs) and a bewildering number of options for those who'd like to end their lives by getting killed by the wildlife. Diving the Great Barrier Reef with a small gaggle of nervously giggling scuba enthusiasts, most of whom were outwardly excited and inwardly terrified, we were sternly lectured by a muscle bound *god* who was doubling as an instructor. Down there, he insisted, pointing over the side of the bobbing boat, as if we didn't know where 'down there' was, down there we would meet sharks (which would hopefully not start giving thanks for food when they sighted us), rock fish (which park themselves on the ocean floor, disguise themselves as boulders, and then inflict horrible pain on anyone unlucky enough to tread on them) and the infamous box jellyfish. Our dive instructor had obviously missed his calling, and should have worked as a producer of terrifying slasher movies, because he relished the opportunity to scare the living daylights out of us. Apparently the sting of the box jellyfish is so excruciatingly painful that there have been those who have managed to struggle out of the water after being attacked by these tiny predators, but they then screamed and begged those who tried to help them to shoot them dead. Mmmm. This didn't sound like an attractive element of our dive. No wonder we were all cocooned in anti-jellyfish suits, which covered just about every inch of our flesh. As we bobbed around in the swell, seconds from submerging, I wanted to cry for my mother, explaining between sobs that it had all been a terrible mistake and that I couldn't swim, and get into the boat and therefore place plenty of distance between me and the monsters that were quietly waiting for me down there in the depths. I didn't. I went on the dive. And yes, we did see some sharks, but they, helpfully, had recently lunched and so showed no interest in snacking.

Then there was the close encounter of a brown snake kind. Strolling by a lake in a town, I mistakenly thought that snakes wouldn't be found in the area. After all, this was a built up location with a high density of human population: surely they wouldn't allow snakes there. It would be against the rules. They did. We didn't spot it until the last moment, when my wife Kay was just about to step onto the rather well camouflaged creature. The high pitched scream that I erupted into possibly saved her life, and most certainly was a rallying call to all dogs within the local vicinity.

And then there were the multitudinous perils that we faced as we went out for a day safari into the Aussie rainforest. Our friendly guide informed us that there were stinging plants that are quite unlike the mildly anti-social stinging nettles that are found in the UK. These evil triffids pack a punch that is worse than the combined efforts of a bee swarm. Not nice. I asked about spiders, and then immediately wished that I hadn't. There were pizza sized spiders lurking in the trees, whose chosen *modus operandi* was to suddenly drop and land on the face of a hapless passer-by, consigning them to a somewhat surprising and hairy suffocation. And then there are the cassowaries, who like to pursue their prey and then disembowel them with a single stab of a claw. I like my bowels. Laughing nervously, I sought assurance from our guide. 'I'm glad to be out here with someone who knows the country and isn't afraid,' I ventured, hopefully. His reply was less than comforting. 'Not afraid? I often lose sleep before coming out here, there are so many dangers' he said, looking this way and that in a way that was most disconcerting. Suddenly my bowels felt vulnerable.

And so Australia is beautiful, fun, sociable, and terrifyingly perilous, because there are so many creatures that can bite, sting, stab, smother or simply swallow you whole, as in the case of the great white shark.

But I was yet to come across another peril that would cause me even more terror, and looking back, I still feel wobbly as I remember the encounter. The creature was about four foot six inches tall. It was a female of the species. It had a somewhat terrifying reputation. And it wore a uniform. And a smile. Bizarrely, this creature is often seen brandishing a tambourine.

She was – and is – a Salvation Army officer. Scratch that. Think Pope, or the Archbishop of Canterbury. General Eva Burrows is retired now, but as former leader of the world's Salvationists, she occupied the highest rank they could bestow upon her. A stunningly impressive lady, she is confident, formidable even, but very kind. A sprightly eighty-four years of age, she was spotted as a leader in her formative years, becoming prefect and then head girl at her school. Her contribution to Australian life is well known. She's been decorated as a Companion of the Order of Australia, and has no less than five honorary doctorates. When General Eva issues a command, people obey. I know I did.

I was preaching at the final night of the Army conference. I've been privileged to speak at Salvationist events around the world, despite not being connected with the organisation in any way. I don't even like brass instruments that much, but my Salvationist friends and hosts have been wonderfully willing to overlook that. On this particular night, the meeting had gone well, the singing had been 'bright', as Army folks are prone to say, and there was a buzz of real excitement and joy as the evening drew to a close. It was then that it happened. The bite came so quickly, from such an unexpected quarter.

It was General Eva. She'd decided that it was time for a 'glory march'. I'm not sure of the exact purpose of these spontaneous little trips, but Eva decided it was something we should do. People march around the building, up and down the aisles, round and round, as the band plays and the people clap and sing. Perhaps it's a declaration of intention, a parade of war, to show that those marching mean serious business – they want to do some damage to the powers of darkness, and the march says that they're ready to go.

Whatever the precise purpose, Eva was in a marching mood. But I was quite unprepared for the news that she had decided that she, as the General, and me, as the preacher, should be the sole participants in the march, at least at the beginning of it.

Dashing down the aisle at a speed not normally associated with those in their mid-eighties, Eva grabbed my hand, hauled me into the aisle, and hissed, 'Come on, Jeff. Let's march.'

And so I did. My mind was screaming. Should I keep hold of her hand? Should we march or run? She broke into a skip. Should I follow suit? I did, feeling a bit like a schoolboy on a jaunty bop through the park. The congregation laughed and clapped and sang even louder, and we just kept going round and round and round …

And I'm glad I did. It was a delight to bop around with the lovely Eva. And it was awful. Reflecting on the experience afterwards, I realised an unpalatable truth: I spend too much time worrying about what people think of me. Initially, I wanted to refuse the march, but it would have looked wrong, churlish even. And then as we leapt around the place while the band worked themselves into an even greater lather, my mind was screaming: what on earth do I look like, dashing around like a demented dervish? I'm not sure it was pride that fed my thoughts; perhaps it was more like fear. But this I know: I spend way too much energy agitated or speculating about what people think about me.

That's why I went ahead with that shark infested dive. Frankly, I didn't want to. But I did it anyway, and not just because I had paid up front. The thrust is that I was reluctant to call the whole thing off and swim back to the boat like a shamed coward, to meet the disapproval of the crew, who would mutter that the English guy just wasn't man enough ...

Despite the fact that I would likely never, ever see any of them again, I plunged beneath the surface because I was more scared of their verdicts about me than I was of killer jellyfish, or sharks with grumbling stomachs.

The double irony of all this is that most of the time, even though people might form an opinion of us, we never get to find out what it is anyway, because they don't verbalise their thoughts. Their verdict remains unspoken. I'm being driven or paralysed by people whose names I don't know, and I'm speculating about thoughts that they may or may not have. Madness indeed.

And so I'm trying to worry a little less about what others might just possibly be thinking about me. That doesn't mean that I embrace a couldn't-care-less attitude of bullish self-obsession. I don't want to stomp my way through life indifferent about whether I offend or worst still, bruise. I'm not calling for us to be proudly impervious to the feelings of others.

But I do want to stop shadow boxing and playing guessing games about what others think.

Because you don't need a forest full of wild beasts or an ocean crammed with killer marine life in order to be afraid. All that's required is an active imagination, and an obsessive concern about what other people think of us.

17 Dasher is a reindeer's name

For most of us, the yuletide event ushers us into the season to be frantic. That's ironic, because the very first Christmas took place in a more tranquil, pastoral setting, when an angelic big band scared the living daylights out of a herd of shepherds. Sheep watching isn't terribly exhilarating, and those chaps weren't used to sudden supernatural singsongs, seeing as they had the most boring job in the world. But then the night sky lit up with angelic neon, electrifying what had been just another predictable, relatively peaceful night time, and nothing would ever be quite the same.

In the past, my own Christmas preparations have not been so emotionally serene, or exciting.

I remember the tribulation began with the acquisition of the Christmas tree, which is usually portrayed in the movies as a joyous family event, when a group of smiling souls, usually adorned in ridiculous snowman sweaters and fluffy ear-muffs, go in search of the perfect tree. Scrambling around the loft looking for the tired, plastic version isn't nearly as heart-warming, so we opted for the real thing, a poor decision that led to a minor blood-letting. I held up 4,321 trees before we were able to opt for the tree of choice. Okay, it was more likely around a dozen, but I handled enough trees to end up with bleeding hands and a coat that smelled of pine for weeks afterwards.

And then the tree grew at least a foot after I'd purchased it, (a bit like a woodland version of one of those leg lengthening services that used to be all the rage) and so in trying to manoeuvre what looked like a netting-encased corpse into the back of my car, I got repeatedly stabbed by those pesky pine needles, received splinters from the trunk, and then nearly decapitated a cyclist on the way home because wayward branches protruded out of the windows. This elicited a number of expressions of praise and worship (or something like that) from yours truly. Bah, humbug.

And then I had to do battle with the tree stand, which was designed by a crazed inventor who is on a crusade to tempt Christian leaders to swear. One is required to fill the wretched contraption with cold water, and then hold the tree with one hand while simultaneously kneeling before it to twist ill-fitting bolts into the trunk. This resulted in a tilting tree reminiscent of the Leaning Tower of Pisa, and a stand filled with pine needle soup, which of course spilled over onto the carpet. Deep and abiding joy.

Then came the annual ritual of the tree lights, an occasion that I not only fear, but occasionally dream about. Actually, they are nightmares, and for very good reason. Our tree lights are the self-knotting variety. Even though we carefully pack them away when their job is done each year, someone breaks into our loft with the sole agenda of tying them up into insurmountable tangles. The chaotic green jumble of cable is finally untangled, and then we always discover that one of the bulbs doesn't work, and so we insert and remove bulbs, and that string of lights is still dark, nudging us to more potentially naughty muttering. But then, staggeringly, we place that useless string of lights back into its box, which we will retrieve again next year and repeat the same fun ritual: untangle, insert bulbs, remove bulbs, mutter, replace in box ...

It's been said that one definition of insanity is doing the same thing over and over again, and expecting different results. As I place the redundant lights back in their box, muttering to self that it'll be different next year because they will work, I wonder if I have now qualified for official certification: I am truly insane.

But my tree wrestling was not the most stressful or embarrassing event. No, my biggest gaff happened when I drove to the butchers to collect the turkey. It should have been a simple enough task. But not, of course, for me. Nothing ever is.

I placed big bird on the passenger's seat, began my drive home, and suddenly a warning light came on, accompanied by a shrill beeping noise. It was the seatbelt warning signal.

The car has a built in sensor in each seat, and detects that a passenger is present, but that a seatbelt has not be fastened. My friend the turkey only weighed about twenty pounds, but nevertheless, my car was insistent: I was carrying an unsecured passenger. Despite the fact that this particular passenger was half frozen, decapitated and very dead, and therefore would have been quite unaffected by a swift flight through my windscreen, the car warning system continued to protest. Loudly.

I know. I could have simply pulled over and placed the turkey on the floor of the car, the simplest and most obvious solution. But I reached across, grabbed the seatbelt, and strapped that turkey in. I believe I am the only man in the UK who chauffeur-drives seatbelt protected dead birds. And all because I didn't pause to think.

Thoughtlessness. That's why I didn't measure the tree, wear protective gloves while putting it in the car, secure wayward branches, or fill the stand with water *after* securing the tree. That's why I lobbed the defunct tree lights back in their box, instead of in the bin. And that's why I strapped in a frozen bird. Because I didn't pause long enough to think.

In the baubles and blur that is Christmas, we can so easily miss the point of it all, because Dasher has become our name, borrowed from a reindeer. It's been said that, on all gravestones, there is one thing shared, whatever the specific details of the deceased – and that's the dash.

John Smith, 9 April 1903 – 6 January 1983. Eighty years or so. But there's still the dash.

Sarah Giles, 7 March 1960 – 24 May 1980. Just two

decades. A quicker dash than most.

Life is a dash, never more so than at Christmas.

In our fervent hunt for the right pair of socks for Uncle Sid or slippers for Auntie Vera, we neglect to think about the fact that Christmas means wondrous, international rescue by the God who refused to just watch us from a distance. Our world is not an abandoned planet, spinning in lonely space. We are a visited people. Christ has come. Give yourself the luxurious gift of ten minutes to ponder that wonderful truth. Unpack it with gratitude.

And just as Christmas came first to those on the margins – shepherding was a chosen occupation for rascals – so the message of peace and joy includes those who, through no fault of their own, have nothing under the tree, and indeed no tree at all. Let's think and plan and give, lest Christmas become a love feast of self-indulgence. And let's think too about those who find the season quite unbearable, who are mugged by nostalgia mingled with despair, as they look back and ache for better, bygone days, when smiles and songs were shared with loved ones now departed, and greatly missed. Let's notice, and think hard about how we might take some joy their way. It can be done, and it might not take very much.

18 Love the ones you're with

Growing up means that you are supposed to leave childish behaviour behind. I think I've largely succeeded, and if you disagree I just won't play with you anymore, so there.

Seriously, I think I've developed a modicum of maturity. If I'm offered food that isn't to my liking, I no longer decorate someone's head with it, which does make for a much better experience in restaurants. And I no longer scream a deafening wail in the key of G when I'm upset. That would be very silly. The key of C is *so* much better. But there's one childhood habit that I've not been able to grow out of, and it's about time.

It *is* about time, literally. Sometimes I'd like to suspend time. Extend the life of that spectacular sunset. Stretch that laugh-out-loud evening with friends so that it lasts a week, so I could lob another dozen logs on the fireplace, sip another glass of wine, and savour the warm smiles again and again.

It's always been that way with me. As a child, I would go to the fair, luxuriate in the colliding smells of fried onions and candy floss, and then hop on one of those garishly painted merry-go-rounds. You know – the ones with the slightly off-tune organ and the clashing cymbals. But as soon as the ride edged slowly into motion, and I'd wave goodbye to Mum for the twenty seconds it took to go around once, I'd edge into worry: how much time had I got left to enjoy this experience? Would the scowling chap with the ponytail and bad tattoos who was controlling the ride give me my full quota of time to enjoy being astride the wooden horse with impossibly large teeth? As soon as I began the experience, I whittled away about it coming to an end, all too soon. The merry on my merry-go-round was spoiled because I was preoccupied with fear that it would go round too quickly.

I really enjoyed the movie *About Time*. Featuring the stunning Bill Nighy, it told the story of a family in which any male could pop into a small dark space such as a wardrobe, clench their fists, and pop back to a previous moment in their lifetime and enjoy it all over again. I loved the film, because I have no aspirations for a *Back to the Future* trip back into Henry the Eighth's court. I'd probably end up witnessing to Anne Boleyn, which would be mistaken for flirtation by His Royal Highness, leading to a very radical haircut, starting at my neck. But I'd love to just revisit and relive moments of my own *personal* history.

And I've been guilty of taking the same attitude towards

some of the nicer times in my more recent life. Blessed with a lovely holiday, I spent much of it wondering (a) how many days of bliss we had left and (b) was this my last experience of this place? My joy was tainted because I fretted endlessly about it ending.

That doesn't mean that we shouldn't look ahead, plan, prepare, and even dream. But there comes a point when planning for the future becomes preoccupation with it, or when nostalgia for what *was* ruins our capacity to celebrate what *is*.

Paul Tournier famously said that most people spend their whole lives indefinitely preparing to live. I don't want to daydream through my days, mentally elsewhere. I want to be fully present and be in the moment, now.

And this business of being there is not just about time. Go into any restaurant and you're likely to find a table full of people who are there in body, but elsewhere in soul. Fixated with devices, instead of being present, they are tweeting or Facebook-ing someone else.

And here's a reminder of what we all know about social networking: unless you're extremely selective, those hundreds or thousands of 'friends' on Facebook are not our friends. They won't be snacking on the sausage rolls at the bash that follows our funeral. But if you half-listen to the people that you're with while concentrating on the souls that you'll never meet, your actual friendships will go offline at high speed. Don't miss out on engaging with interesting, colourful, needy, inspiring people in favour of the faceless (apart from a dodgy profile photo) on Facebook.

Life was meant to be about conversation, not a newsflash. Twitter is most often about declaration rather than conversation. But life was never meant to be a series of pithy pronouncements made in 140 characters or less. Don't issue a press release: have a real chat instead.

And your phone won't feel hurt if you ignore it.

I have a friend who is wise, loving and a brilliant listener – until his phone rings, beeps or chirps. He is then compelled to answer it, even though he might be in a critical conversation with someone who is sharing a marriage crisis, a major career change, or a forthcoming amputation. There might be a person on your phone, but your phone is not a person. Take control. Be the boss. Ignore it. Being a machine, it won't get wounded, feel neglected, or withdraw into a sulky silence, not talking to you for three days. Believe me; it'll be ready to talk again whenever you are.

And you don't need a technology addiction to be absent. Have you ever felt the humiliation of talking to someone who is rather obviously looking over your shoulder, searching for someone more interesting? I have. It's horrible. I'd rather be ignored completely than be treated to the agony of trying to chat with someone who isn't even pretending to engage with me.

Jesus was a popular party guest, and not just because He was rather good with wine. Whether it was lunch with Danny DeVito in a tree (Zacchaeus), fussing over children clamouring for a cuddle of blessing, or chatting with a well-side wanton woman in the sweltering heat of noon, He was *there*, asking questions, listening, noticing. Those who tried to hustle Him away from those vital encounters received a swift telling off. The whole incarnation story says this: God saw. He came. And He stayed, by His Spirit. And now, in a way that I honestly can't fathom, we are assured of His full attention.

Here's some very poor advice when it comes to intimacy: 'love the one you're with'. It's a recipe for divorce, heartache and some rather itchy diseases. But it's a good mantra for friendship. When with those you value, ignore those who are demanding your attention via phone or pesky social media: love the ones you're with, and especially when life is good, love the moment you're in, because, in a moment, it will be gone.

19 Be nice to your vicar

Over the years and because of the miles I've travelled, I've come in contact with a lot of vicars, priests, elders and pastors. I've met selfless, hard working souls who pour out their lives for their churches and communities, and I've met lazy ministers who would make a sloth look productive. I've bumped into breathtakingly gifted entrepreneurs who would have made millions if they hadn't chosen their vocation, and others who are 'in the ministry' mainly because they can't do anything else too well, and don't do ministry that well either. I've met servant hearted types whose ideal night out would be to gird up their loins with a towel, grab a bowl and head for a local foot washing, and power hungry bullies who need to be taken behind the bike sheds and shown what bullying really looks and feels like.

I know. I'm biased because I'm a pastor, and given the choice between engaging with pleasant, encouraging, smiling souls, and those carping critics who make piranhas look like tame goldfish, I'd obviously choose the former. But it's worth thinking about *why* we should be nice to the women and men who lead us, for one simple reason: encouragement takes thought and strategy, and shouldn't just happen because it just happens. Years ago Ian Dury (together with his Blockhead friends) sang about 'Reasons to be cheerful'. Here are five reasons to be nice to your local leader:

They frequently take the blame for God

It's true: Christian leaders represent God, who is currently invisible, and, at times, seems unavailable, especially when things go horribly wrong in life. When people get angry with God, unfortunately there's no customer support line to call, so they frequently take out their frustration on the person they most associate with God, which might be their vicar, pastor, leader or priest. Getting slapped on behalf of the Almighty is not a happy experience. If you're mad with God, include a rant in your prayers, because He can cope, being God. But your local leader is not quite as resilient. If you think they're thick skinned and can take it on the chin, you're probably wrong. The reason they got into that vocation is often because they are sensitive souls who genuinely care. And being the vicar, when they get mad with God because God's people get mad with them, they have no one to slap. Nobody human, anyway.

They are required to say some things that they'd prefer not to say

The Bible contains some awkward truths, and if your pastor

is going to be faithful in preaching it, they'll have to deal with some tricky passages on sensitive subjects like divorce, war, adultery, sexuality, and, brace yourself for the subject that tends to light the blue touchpaper, money. When speaking on these subjects, they are unlikely to please all of the people all of the time, which means they will take some heat. Cool them down with some kindness. When they tackle those controversial issues, they are demonstrating bravery, not bullishness. If they make a statement you disagree with, let it get under your skin, circle your brain, fuel your prayers, and even challenge your heart, before you send that vociferous email. Come to think of it, cancel the vociferous email.

They are often the target for gossip

In some churches, Christians don't gossip, they share. Under that guise of sharing, 'Please pray for the pastor, he/she is really struggling right now', we can give the impression that the pastor is struggling with faith and is now a fully paid up member of the Humanist Society, struggling with temptation, and has opened their own private harem, or is struggling with anger towards his congregation, and is now a serial killer whose crime pattern is striking during the after-church cup of tea while wearing clerical attire. Gossip destroys people. Don't pass it on.

They don't have a hotline to God

Some think that their pastors have a VIP pass to the courts of heaven, and begin each day with a happy little chat with God. They don't. They too struggle with doubt, unanswered prayer, and when going through wilderness times in their faith, often have to appear more certain than they are, not because they are faking it, but because it is inappropriate for them to dump their own private struggles on their congregation every Sunday. If you sometimes feel that your prayer life is a struggle, know that they frequently feel the same. These days I'm more concerned about those who insist that God and they have interference-free conversations than I am about the souls who fear that their connection is patchy at best.

They usually don't have a cunning plan for world dominion
Okay, there *are* some wolves out there masquerading as shepherds. There are power hungry, authoritarian clerical control freaks who would be better at leading a fascist regime than a local congregation. Spiritual abuse *does* happen, and it's very serious indeed. Some leaders do have a well-proven weapon that efficiently silences anyone with a brain cell who asks awkward questions: they just say that these people are being divisive, an excellent device for manipulation and control. But be aware that the vast majority of leaders are ordinary people (God only uses ordinary folk, nothing else is available), who are simply doing their best to respond to a vocational call to help people to discover Jesus.

So go ahead. Make their day, and help them out by being nice.

20 Larry & Maggie T

In the late 1970s, the world was in the grip of a fashion demon that roamed the earth. Otherwise sensible people adorned themselves in the most grotesque garb, stupefied into believing that super-sized flares looked cool. We sweated profusely in foul fabrics like Bri-Nylon and Crimplene; I sported a hairstyle with a bouffant that stuck out like Florida, tempting children and small animals to shelter beneath its shade. Glam rockers like Slade were anything but glam, video recorders were ultra-high tech, and the nation was about to be hit by a feminine force that, for good or ill, changed just about everything, as Margaret Thatcher, handbag on arm, marched into Number Ten. This was the era of the intimidating giant called Mr T, who had muscles in places where I don't have places. But compared with *Mrs* T, he was a wimp.

Death didn't put an end to her electioneering. Within hours of her passing, she was the subject of yet another vote, this time in a West End theatre. *Billy Elliot the Musical* contains a scene where a huge inflatable Thatcher fills the stage, accompanied by a song that joyfully anticipates her death. Before the performance began the audience were asked to decide if the song should be included that night, seeing as she was so recently departed. It was a landslide defeat. Only three voted against its inclusion, so the song went ahead as usual. And speaking of songs, the BBC fretted about whether to play *Ding–Dong! The Witch is Dead* on their Radio One chart show.

Ironically, the Iron Lady would probably have approved of the straight talk about her legacy. Famous for her withering glare and her inability to suffer fools gladly, she never craved hollow popularity, and was even nervous when her party scored too high in the midterm opinion polls. Like all of us, she was deeply flawed, often wrong in her insistence that she was right. Saint Margaret she certainly was not. And death should never place anyone beyond appropriate critical evaluation of their life's work.

But the partying that took place around her passing was further evidence of a famine of respect in our culture. Perhaps I'd feel differently if I lived in one of the devastated mining communities that bore the brunt of her policies, but surely it's inhumane to dance on anyone's grave, not least because it's tantamount to spitting on the grief of their family members. While nobody should be forced to mourn, those who do mourn should be blessed, not cursed with guilt by association.

Bitterness is never satisfying. It never brings resolution or closure. Ongoing rage shows that our souls are still deeply stained; we remain under the power of the person we hate.

Their shadow lingers, and we live under it. And it achieves little or nothing. Thatcher is dead. She is impervious to any insults that might be rained down upon her. The vitriolic might find greater joy in putting their energies into doing something practical to correct the current ills, of which there are plenty.

And bitterness blinds us to any strengths that a person has. Love her or loath her, she *was* a leader. As a church leader I'm challenged by the need for bravery. At times I'm afraid to speak out on controversial issues or make awkward decisions, concerned with the consensus rather than the kingdom.

Perhaps for some the wound is too deep, and that it's unreasonable to call for grace and dignity. And then I think of Larry, a quiet unassuming chap in our church, whose life was changed for ever by the phone call that every parent fears. His daughter had been murdered by her boyfriend. Larry trudged a painful pathway, ultimately being able to forgive his child's killer. This was no quick, 'Nescafé forgiving', but a determined journey to offer grace that is nothing short of amazing. Larry aches every day for his lost little girl, but doesn't have to stagger under the additional weight of unresolved hatred. In the end, vengeful rejoicing is uglier than any bizarre 1970s fashion choice. Give me platform shoes or Crimplene flares over bitterness any day.

I know. There will be those who will insist that I can't begin to imagine the pain experienced by some, and they're absolutely right.

So don't take my word for it. Take it from Larry.

21 Let us pray

I've never been much good at prayer. Perhaps I need to join a group. 'Hi. My name is Jeff, and I'm addicted to activity. And conversation.'

'Hi Jeff ...', the group responds in unison. Hopefully.

So while time alone (anything less than an hour) is surely helpful, for me, extended solitude quickly becomes solitary confinement. As a wilderness hermit, dedicated to prayer and a diet of grass and goat droppings, I'd be rubbish.

Even the mention of the word 'prayer' intimidates me, and I'm not alone. Most of us labour under the impression that everybody else is better at praying than we are. This feeling is compounded if you've ever read a book written by one of those bionic mystics or saints who, 300 years before there was anything on the telly, would pop off to the woods, crawl into the bowels of a log, and have six blissful weeks of fasting and prayer with apparently zero effort. I could never aspire to such dizzy heights. I'd probably give myself to twenty minutes of fervent prayer before exiting the log hastily to (a) remove errant woodlice from my underwear and (b) break my gruelling twenty minute fast by demolishing a double cheeseburger.

Perhaps you feel the same way, and so maybe we should adjust our thinking about prayer? First, Scripture freely acknowledges that we will find prayer tough, so if we're challenged, we're not bad, just human. 'We do not know what we ought to pray for' (Rom. 8:26) says the mighty apostle in a confession that nudges me to head-butt a tambourine in gratitude. I so appreciate Paul's honesty in acknowledging that talking with someone who is invisible isn't that easy. And then the pages of the Bible frequently portray people struggling to pray – and falling asleep as they tried. Jesus' disciples (hand-picked to change world history, remember) drifted off into exhausted slumber no less than three times in the Garden of Gethsemane, even though Jesus had specifically asked them to stay awake, alert and do vigil with Him. The thought of them snoring their way through one of the most epic junction moments of all time (a habit of theirs, they got sleepy during the transfiguration too) fills me with hope.

As for lengthy prayer times, I'm encouraged that Jesus countered the Pharisaic idea that the only good prayers were long prayers. We might need to pray at length, but we don't have to set a meter running. Here's a thought: it's better to pray for five minutes a day, than it is to *believe* that you're supposed to pray for an hour a day, but not actually pray at all.

I'm trying to be more practical about prayer too. Shared prayer with another is good, and easier, but strangely sometimes doesn't feel like it truly counts as much as the solo variety, which is odd, seeing as we're specifically instructed to agree in prayer, which obviously involves others. And then I like to go for a walk when I pray. Not only does this double the benefits, giving me a physical workout as well as the opportunity for time with God, but I've discovered that it's fairly difficult to drift off to sleep while walking. Not many people slump to the ground in slumber while trotting along the high street.

And as a non-Anglican, I've found liturgy useful at times. Sometimes I use *Common Worship* as a foundation for my prayers, mainly because there are times when I can't think of too much that is useful to say, and quickly get bored with the sound of my own voice.

It's a bit odd though, because it's designed for congregational use, which means that there are parts for the priest to say, and responses required from the people.

I do both bits.

'The peace of the Lord be with you,' I say to myself.

'And also with you,' I respond to myself.

But I've found a way to feel less silly about this. I use different voices.

A little odd, I agree. *And so do I.*

22 At the moment

I was always terrible at French at school. I was rather terrified of my teacher, Mr Peckett (I jest not), who used to deal with any misbehaving pupils by whacking them with a slipper. I'm not saying that I was given to classroom naughtiness, but I went through a phase when I probably had a rubber imprint of a shoe sole on my backside. I used to amuse myself by lobbing orange pips (does anyone remember them?) around the classroom, hence the regular thrashings. Now I can throw an orange pip with precision, but my French language skills are somewhat limited, which means that, in French, I can ask the time, say yes, no, hello, thank you, and Eiffel Tower.

But there is also one French phrase that has stuck in my head through the years, and that is, 'Which is the way to the railway station?' (I said I could remember how to say it, not write it, so you'll have to trust me.) How I have longed for the day when I could utilise this precious part of my education.

Whenever I have been in France, I have hoped that I'd find myself with the need to ask someone where the station was, but, alas, the opportunity has never arisen. This has been because either (a) much as I'd like to deny it, I knew exactly where the station was, or (b) I was driving, so I didn't need to know the station's whereabouts, not being in need of a train. And then there was the added problem that, even if I actually needed to locate the station, and I managed to parrot the question in flawless French, I wouldn't understand the reply anyway, which makes the asking a big waste of time. I've never been able to use my precious phrase.

That is, until today, in London. A couple of French students approached me and asked, in very broken English, the way to a street in Victoria. With delight, I suddenly realised that this was my moment, when I could actually utilise the phrase, 'the way to the railway station', because the street in question was right next to it. Thirty-four years after learning it, this was finally my big opportunity. Delighted, I opened my mouth to reply, and promptly forgot the phrase. I mumbled something in a garbled combination of French and English, the exact translation of which was probably, 'Turn left at the/what is the time, please, and then right at the Eiffel Tower/thank you/no/hello'. They smiled and were polite, but I could see that they believed me to be in need of professional help. They moved on, and I missed the moment I had been prepared for over three decades earlier. Rats.

More seriously, I've wondered if I've missed other, much more significant moments. C.S. Lewis taught that, for the Christian, there are no such things as chance encounters or lucky breaks. To use his phrase, he saw behind the unfolding minutes of our lives that 'a secret Master of the Ceremonies has been at work'[1]. That doesn't mean that I need to be paralysed, only able to pop down to Tesco or Sainsbury's for the fish fingers after a time of prayer and fasting. But it does mean that I need to do life with my eyes open, ready to make the most of every opportunity, and especially prepared for junction moments: decision times that might shape a decade, or a lifetime.

A decision made in a second can be like a rudder that turns a huge ship.

Of course, the problem is that we don't know which days are the turning point days. Opportunity, like temptation, doesn't book an appointment or call ahead.

Today could be one of 'those' days. So let's pray that God will give us wisdom when a moment arrives. And if you'd like directions to a railway station in France, then I'm your man.

[1] C.S. Lewis, *The Four Loves* (1960).

NATIONAL DISTRIBUTORS

UK: (and countries not listed below)

CWR, Waverley Abbey House, Waverley Lane, Farnham, Surrey GU9 8EP.
Tel: (01252) 784700 Outside UK (44) 1252 784700 Email: mail@cwr.org.uk

AUSTRALIA: KI Entertainment, Unit 21 317-321 Woodpark Road, Smithfield,
New South Wales 2164 Tel: 1 800 850 777 Fax: 02 9604 3699
Email: sales@kientertainment.com.au

CANADA: David C Cook Distribution Canada, PO Box 98, 55 Woodslee Avenue, Paris,
Ontario N3L 3E5 Tel: 1800 263 2664 Email: joy.kearley@davidccook.ca

GHANA: Challenge Enterprises of Ghana, PO Box 5723, Accra
Tel: (021) 222437/223249 Fax: (021) 226227 Email: ceg@africaonline.com.gh

HONG KONG: Cross Communications Ltd, 11/F Ko's House, 577 Nathan Road,
Kowloon Tel: 2780 1188 Fax: 2770 6229 Email: cross@crosshk.com

INDIA: Crystal Communications, Plot No. 125, Road No. 7, T.M.C, Mahendra Hills,
East Marredpally, Secunderabad - 500026 Tel/Fax: (040) 27737145
Email: crystal_edwj@rediffmail.com

KENYA: Keswick Books and Gifts Ltd, PO Box 10242-00400, Nairobi
Tel: (020) 2226047/312639 Email: sales.keswick@africaonline.co.ke

MALAYSIA: Canaanland Distributors Sdn Bhd, No. 25 Jalan PJU 1A/41B, NZX
Commercial Centre, Ara Jaya, 47301 Petaling Jaya, Selangor
Tel: (03) 7885 0540/1/2 Fax: (03) 7885 0545 Email: info@canaanland.com.my

Salvation Publishing & Distribution Sdn Bhd, 23 Jalan SS 2/64, 47300 Petaling Jaya,
Selangor Tel: (03) 78766411/78766797 Fax: (03) 78757066/78756360
Email: info@salvationbookcentre.com

NEW ZEALAND: KI Entertainment, Unit 21 317-321 Woodpark Road, Smithfield,
New South Wales 2164, Australia Tel: 0 800 850 777 Fax: +612 9604 3699
Email: sales@kientertainment.com.au

NIGERIA: FBFM, Helen Baugh House, 96 St Finbarr's College Road, Akoka, Lagos
Tel: (+234) 01-7747429, 08075201777, 08186337699, 08154453905
Email: fbfm_1@yahoo.com

PHILIPPINES: OMF Literature Inc, 776 Boni Avenue, Mandaluyong City
Tel: (02) 531 2183 Fax: (02) 531 1960 Email: gloadlaon@omflit.com

SINGAPORE: Alby Commercial Enterprises Pte Ltd, 95 Kallang Avenue #04-00,
AIS Industrial Building, 339420 Tel: (+65) 629 27238 Fax: (+65) 629 27235
Email: marketing@alby.com.sg

SOUTH AFRICA: Life Media & Distribution, Unit 20, Tungesten Industrial Park,
7 C R Swart Drive, Strydompark 2125 Tel: (+27) 0117924277
Fax: (+27) 0117924512 Email: orders@lifemedia.co.za

SRI LANKA: Christombu Publications (Pvt) Ltd, Bartleet House, 65 Braybrooke Place,
Colombo 2 Tel: (+941) 2421073/2447665 Email: christombupublications@gmail.com

USA: David C Cook Distribution Canada, PO Box 98, 55 Woodslee Avenue, Paris,
Ontario N3L 3E5, Canada Tel: 1800 263 2664 Email: joy.kearley@davidccook.ca

CWR is a Registered Charity – Number 294387
CWR is a Limited Company registered in England – Registration Number 1990308

Other titles by
Jeff Lucas

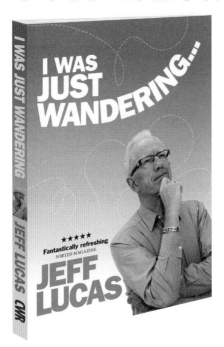

I Was Just Wandering...

There's a lot to kick-start the heart and mind as Jeff describes some embarrassing mishaps and laugh-out-loud episodes from his own experiences. He reminds us that we all have thoughts and struggles that can taunt and torment, but offers relief and reminds us that we're not alone.

ISBN: 978-1-85345-850-7

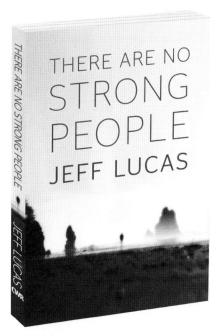

There Are No Strong People

**Is it possible to be hugely blessed by God
and still make a mess of your life?** In this
provocative, breathtakingly honest book on the
Bible's infamous character, Samson, Jeff Lucas
explores some vital principles for living life well.
ISBN: 978-1-85345-624-4

Continue transforming your daily walk with God.

Our compact, daily Bible reading notes for adults are published bimonthly and offer a focus for every need. They are available as individual issues or annual subscriptions, in print, in eBook format or by email.

Life Every Day

Apply the Bible to life each day with these challenging life-application notes written by international speaker and well-known author Jeff Lucas.
64-page booklets, 120x170mm

Every Day with Jesus

With around half a million readers, this insightful devotional by Selwyn Hughes is one of the most popular daily Bible reading tools in the world. A large-print edition is also available.
72-page booklets, 120x170mm

Inspiring Women Every Day

Written by women for women of all ages and from all walks of life. These notes will help to build faith and bring encouragement and inspiration to the lives and hearts of Christian women.
64-page booklets, 120x170mm

Cover to Cover Every Day

Study one Old Testament and one New Testament book in depth with each issue, and a psalm every weekend. Covers every book of the Bible in five years.
64-page booklets, 120x170mm

For current price and to order visit **www.cwr.org.uk/subscriptions**
Also available online or from Christian bookshops

Courses and seminars

Waverley Abbey College

Publishing and media

Conference facilities

Transforming lives

CWR's vision is to enable people to experience personal transformation through applying God's Word to their lives and relationships.

Our Bible-based training and resources help people around the world to:
- Grow in their walk with God
- Understand and apply Scripture to their lives
- Resource themselves and their church
- Develop pastoral care and counselling skills
- Train for leadership
- Strengthen relationships, marriage, family life and much more.

Our insightful writers provide daily Bible-reading notes and other resources for all ages, and our experienced course designers and presenters have gained an international reputation for excellence and effectiveness.

CWR's Training and Conference Centres in Surrey and East Sussex, England, provide excellent facilities in idyllic settings – ideal for both learning and spiritual refreshment.

CWR Applying God's Word
to everyday life and relationships

CWR, Waverley Abbey House,
Waverley Lane, Farnham,
Surrey GU9 8EP, UK

Telephone: **+44 (0)1252 784700**
Email: **info@cwr.org.uk**
Website: **www.cwr.org.uk**

Registered Charity No 294387
Company Registration No 1990308